A WORKING COSTUME DESIGNER'S GUIDE TO COLOR

T0386596

A Working Costume Designer's Guide to Color provides readers with the skills and knowledge to create coherent color schemes for costumes.

Drawing on decades of experience in the costume shop, the author guides readers through every step of the process, from finding inspiration for a color scheme and successfully working with the design team to understanding how lighting design can affect costume color choices. Filled with step-by-step illustrations of how to add colors to a set of renderings and color-block samples to illustrate color theory, terminology, and usage of colors, the book covers a wide range of topics, including:

- How to add colors to a set of renderings to clarify characters and character relationships.
- How color interacts with surface pattern and fabric textures.
- Color theory and terminology.
- How to combine colors to make a coherent color scheme using different methods, including using dominant, supporting, and accent colors.
- How to flatter actors while staying within an overall color scheme.
- Color meanings in different cultures and for different time periods.
- How to manage costume changes to preserve or extend a color scheme.

A valuable resource for students of costume design courses and professional costume designers, *A Working Costume Designer's Guide to Color* provides readers with the tools to create harmonious color schemes that will enhance the look of a production as a whole.

Jeanette deJong is Associate Professor of Costume Design and Technology at the University of Oregon. A member of United Scenic Artists, she has been designing costumes and teaching costume design since 1984. Her professional design credits include shows at Cincinnati Playhouse in the Park, Indiana Repertory Theatre, Williamstown Theatre Festival, Actors' Theatre of Louisville, Oregon Contemporary Theatre, Utah Shakespeare Festival, and Illinois Shakespeare Festival, among many other theatres.

A WORKING COSTUME DESIGNER'S GUIDE TO COLOR

Jeanette deJong

Routledge
Taylor & Francis Group

NEW YORK AND LONDON

First published 2021
by Routledge
605 Third Avenue, New York, NY 10158

and by Routledge
2 Park Square, Milton Park, Abingdon, Oxon, OX14 4RN

Routledge is an imprint of the Taylor & Francis Group, an informa business

Library of Congress Cataloging-in-Publication Data
A catalog record for this title has been requested

ISBN: 978-0-8153-5216-7 (hbk)
ISBN: 978-0-8153-5215-0 (pbk)
ISBN: 978-1-351-13143-8 (ebk)

Typeset in Bembo
by Deanta Global Publishing Services Chennai India

CONTENTS

ACKNOWLEDGMENTS

A most heartfelt *thank you* to the people who have helped me along the way to creating this book:

- Owen Saffell and Charlie Saffell-deJong, for their love and support.
- Lucia Accorsi, for her patience.
- Janet Rose, for generously sharing her lighting design knowledge.

And, especially, *thank you* to all of the directors, costume shop managers, costume technicians, and students who have shared their artistry with me.

INTRODUCTION

I have been a theatre costume designer, technician, and educator for over 35 years. All three aspects of my background have informed and enriched the other two. As a teacher, I have found that there is a wonderful array of good costume books with terrific chapters, yet there can be missing pieces of practical information when one wants to complete a project.

Focused on a specific subject and shaped by years of experience, this book is intended to be one of those "missing" practical chapters, a resource that can be turned to in order to solve a problem. Often, once designers or technicians are out of school and working, they find that there are gaps in what they need to know to successfully complete a project or assignment, no matter how excellent the program from which they graduated. My goal is to help answer questions that come up once a designer or technician is working and no longer has an instructor available to help them in person.

This book is a reference for working designers. Color can be one of the most exciting elements to use when designing costumes, but it can also be a source of anxiety. Color is a wonderful element that can enhance the look of the production as a whole, both in an individual costume and for an overall costume design. Because color has such an important effect on how the audience perceives characters, a designer may be intimidated and find that choosing colors is a stumbling block.

Using color with confidence and joy is a learnable skill. I started my design life by being afraid to make a statement with color and have ended up eagerly embracing color as a valuable tool. The development in between these two points has been a matter of practice, experimentation, the willingness to analyze what worked well or not and **why**, and a recognition that methods of using color can be taught. Great designers may approach color with an intuitive sense, but their work can be examined by everyone else for clues as to how to use color. By understanding how to utilize color, a more intuitive-seeming and assured approach can be developed by **all** designers.

This book will cover a range of color theories, methods for organizing colors, consideration of how color may illustrate characters and flatter actors, and how to put all this information together to create a successful color presentation.

You may find it useful to read every chapter in order, as there is an intended accrual of information as the chapters follow one another. However, it may be more useful for a working designer to be able to dip in and out of the book in order to find specific information. In that case, you will notice that important words and ideas are presented in **boldface**, that words dealing with color, such as Intensity or Value, have the first letter capitalized much more than in usual usage, and that lists and subheadings are used so that information may be quickly accessed by the reader. Color names are capitalized consistently so that they are easily found.

A variety of color illustrations are presented throughout the book. Many of these are in the form of color blocks used to illustrate a concept, without being specific to particular costume designs. The intent is to show possible approaches that can be transferred to problems that the reader is trying to solve without being specific to particular costume silhouettes or characters. Other illustrations show a combination of costume renderings. In this case, skin and hair colors for the renderings are included as they were in the original productions. In other drawings, the skin and hair colors are left blank in order to draw focus to the costume colors and to avoid specifying character ethnicity. Chapter 14 is accompanied by drawings of a variety of (admittedly European-based) period costumes in order to demonstrate the steps for adding colors to build up a color scheme. Three appendices cover color meanings from different cultures and countries, period-based color preferences, and specifics of lighting design that are helpful to a costume designer.

This book is for you. Please use it as you need in order to help you solve color issues that are getting in your way, to provide inspiration for a new approach to color, or in whatever way makes your work with color more joyous and expressive.

1

COLOR INSPIRATIONS

Color is one of the most exciting tools for designing costumes. Color can shape the way that an audience perceives characters, their relationships, and the style of a production. Color can be used to organize and direct the attention of the audience toward an important character or moment, to underline relationships between characters and groups, and to help clarify when and where the production is being set. Color is a wonderful element that can enhance the look of the production as a whole, apart from the shape or style of the costumes.

Because color is such a strong aspect of design, it can also become a source of anxiety for many designers. At the start of my career, I found a color scheme that had worked for one production – Grey, Black, White, and Mauve – and repeated it in most of my design work for the next several years. This was due to fear of making a mistake and in being acclimated to the grey, misty weather in the region where I grew up.

FIGURE 1.1   Black, Grey, and White color range

It was only when I relocated to a new city with clear light, bright sun, and a culture that used color with joy that I realized that I needed to be bolder and freer in my own use of color. I saw how colors were combined in local fashions, gardens, and architecture and I began to allow myself to expand and experiment with color. Eventually Red, Gold, Green, bright Blue, Purple, other rich hues, and bold contrasts became part of the palette that I could increasingly balance in a design. The more I saw color around me, the more comfortable I felt in using it with confidence in my work.

Given all the colors in the world, how does a designer begin to choose? Inspirations for costume color directions can be everywhere if you choose to look for them. Color ideas can be gleaned from specific images in the script, the typical colors used in the fashion and décor of a time period, the director's sense of the production, a piece of fine or decorative art that a designer responds to and that seems to reflect the play, nature, architecture, cars, or through a serendipitous combination of influences that create a starting point that can be explored. Consider all the sources of inspiration for assembling color schemes and allow yourself to play.

Let's examine some sources of color inspirations.

Script References

As with all costume design choices, start with color images in the **script**.

Some plays contain specific references to color, such as Hamlet's dark mourning clothes. Other plays may elicit such a strong mood that certain colors will support the mood much better than others. For example, Greek tragedies such as *Oedipus Rex* or *Medea* are not generally costumed in bright Pastels or Neon colors, no matter the period in which they are set, but are usually designed with deep, earthy, and restrained colors to match the stately mood of these plays.

FIGURE 1.2 Oedipus Rex, set in late 1940s Europe

FIGURE 1.3   *Romeo and Juliet* colors with a clear difference between the colors used for the two families

It is helpful to be aware of **color traditions** for certain plays, so that the tradition may be consciously used or subverted. *Romeo and Juliet* is often costumed to help organize the two warring families, with clearly different color schemes for the Montagues versus the Capulets. This tradition is even carried over into the modern retelling of the story in *West Side Story*. However, the contrasting color groupings are not actually contained in the script.

Although **expected**, the contrasting colors may not be appropriate for a particular production of *Romeo and Juliet*. If the concept of your production focuses more on the overall society in which the lovers exist, rather than on the strife between the families, the concept might be better expressed through using similar colors but in very different intensities and textures between the families. Knowing the color expectations and traditions for a play can be helpful, but they are not laws that must always be followed. More specifics on choosing colors to reflect character relationships will be discussed in Chapters 3–7 and Chapter 11.

Period Setting

Color schemes can be drawn from the time period suggested by the script, whether that is the time in which the action is placed, the period in which the play was written, or an entirely different period choice that will illuminate the play for a particular production. For example, Moliere's *The Misanthrope*, written during the reign of Louis XIV in France, may suggest the sky Blue, Gold, and White color scheme typical of this period, or use sepia-toned colors. However, David Ives's *School for Lies*, which uses modern rhymes to retell *The Misanthrope*'s story, might be better served by using bold, bright, modern colors along with accurate period costume shapes.

However, a single period color scheme does not necessarily always apply to **all** the costumes in a production. In *The Waiting Room*, three women of different time periods (one of which is from the 1990s) meet in a modern doctor's office waiting room. Each woman's costume might logically reflect the time period and culture that she represents, rather than all of them being united by a common color scheme. Two of the women's husbands are also seen and coordinate with their wife's individual period-inspired colors. The surrounding modern characters, however, could be part of a color scheme that is outside those of the three main women.

FIGURE 1.4 *The Misanthrope*

FIGURE 1.5 *School for Lies*

Following this same idea, for a production of Shakespeare's *Twelfth Night* in which the characters are dressed in costumes from various time periods, based on their individual personalities, each might be costumed in a different color scheme based on their individual time period, and they would need to be balanced with one another to create an overall composition.

Typical color choices for a variety of cultures and time periods are contained in Appendix 2. The colors listed there include fashionable garment colors as well as decorative and architectural colors. Good sources for period colors include artwork and advertising images of different time periods, as well as Owen Jones's *The Grammar of Ornament*, which is a good secondary source of decorative colors up to the late 19th century.

FIGURE 1.6 *The Waiting Room*

FIGURE 1.7 *Twelfth Night.* Bottom register: Orsino in the 1830s Romantic period, Olivia in the 1870s Victorian period, Viola as Cesario in the 1920s. Middle register: Malvolio as a Puritan, Maria as an 1890s beachgoer, Sir Toby as a Cavalier, Sir Andrew as a 1780s fop. Top register: Feste as a modern street person, and Fabian as an early 19th-century waiter

Director's Concept

Directors will often have their own sense of the colors that will be appropriate for a production. This may be shared through artwork that the director presents to the design team, through key words for the tone of the production such as "war-torn" or "silly" or "nostalgic," or through the proposed style of the production such as "abstract" or "comic" or "realistic." During the initial discussions with the director, bring samples of **your** take on the colors suggested both by the script – whether from specific script references or the overall mood of the play – and by the time period of the script. As key words or script references may conjure different color images for different people, it is valuable to bring some color chips or samples with you to look at together and discuss early in the design process.

For example, "war-torn" may suggest an overall subdued color as the base, with slashes of dirtied, darker colors or areas of Red. This may be contrasted with cleaner areas of military-derived colors, for the army and/or supporters of the ruling regime.

"Silly" color schemes may contain bold contrasts with larger areas of bright color. Added bands of edging, graphic patterns, or color break-ups can add more visual movement.

Finally, "nostalgic" productions may use warm colors, with a range of tones to indicate a range of character ages. Light colors around faces (such as collars) and dark colors for shoes, belts, neckties, jackets, coats, and accessories will add interest by expanding the color scheme to include light tints and dark shades. Add some cool colors to create variety in what can otherwise become an undefined mass of beige.

In all cases, if you or the director are using descriptive words to describe the color mood, it is helpful to have color sources with you to consult in early

FIGURE 1.8 *Macbeth* with a war–torn color scheme

FIGURE 1.9   *Servant of Two Masters* with a bright color scheme for a silly effect

FIGURE 1.10   *Into the Woods*

FIGURE 1.11   *The Trestle at Pope Lick Creek* with a nostalgic color scheme

meetings in order to define what is meant by any key words. I have several books of color samples that I bring to the first production meeting for all shows. Even if the colors for the production change as the design process goes on, it is helpful to be able to have a concrete reference to react to when discussing initial color ideas. For more on color categories, see Chapter 5.

If you, as a costume designer, have strong feelings about color choices, bring them forward and discuss how these choices will support the character interpretations and concept. If you don't, take what your collaborators have offered and start from that point. Color will be a matter of negotiation and development as fabrics and garments are gathered to create a costume design. For more discussion of how your collaborators' work will affect costume colors, see Chapter 2.

Color from a Visual Reference

Artwork and photographs are great sources for creating a color scheme. Analyzing artworks such as well-known paintings, decorative sources such as fabric prints or ceramics or interior designs, or even period advertisements, can be a starting point from which to extract colors.

If you find a visual source that feels right for a production, pull the major colors from the source. Be sure to duplicate the color Intensity and Value, and take note of the Proportion of each color in the source, in order to fully replicate the mood of the original artwork. More discussion of visual sources for color inspiration is contained in Chapter 9.

Nature as Inspiration

Nature is sometime referred to as the "Master Design Teacher." Nature provides many wonderful examples of colors used in combination. Fall foliage, a handful of rocks from the beach, or a flower garden may be the inspiration for costume colors. Natural colors tend to have variations of tone, texture, and color intensity even within a single tree, rock, plant, or field. On a sunny fall day, tree foliage may appear Red or Yellow but is really a **spectrum** of rich tones of Red, Orange, Brown, and Yellow, with a background of the Blue sky to set off the brighter colors and to unify all the hues.

Nature-inspired, variegated colors can also be contrasted with solid flat colors such as the concrete, paint, brick, and glass of human-made architecture to make a point of the opposition of nature and society. Shakespeare's *A Midsummer Night's Dream* contrasts the restrictive royal court against the freedom of nature as counterpoints in the play, and the costume design for this play may use opposing types of colors – flat vs. mottled – to illustrate different character groups.

When developing a Nature-based color scheme, be sure to work with the scenic designer, as their choice of background color needs to be factored into the costume color choices. A large sky area will absorb Blue costumes, but will enhance warm or brighter colors. A tonal Brown, Tan, and Olive costume color scheme will disappear if the set architecture is made up of Browns and Tans. Be sure to exchange color swatches with the set designer, keep track of what colors the set is actually being painted (colors on a small chip tend to look very different when painted on a large surface), and add stronger accents to the costumes to keep them from being overwhelmed by the scenery. Although the background color will **always** have an impact on costume colors, because nature feels so

FIGURE 1.12   Autumn trees

FIGURE 1.13   *A Midsummer Night's Dream* costumes contrasting City (left) and Nature (right) color schemes

familiar to us, it can be easy to forget the impact that a large scenic area of sky or woods will have on a group of costumes onstage.

Color Schemes Derived from What Is Available

Being able to develop a costume color scheme completely from the script and the director's concept is a luxury. Often, the costume design needs to incorporate costumes from stock – your stock and what is available to rent or borrow – what is available to purchase, and the fabric sources available. Whether the garments are pulled, rented, purchased, or built, a unifying color of fabric or trim may be used with existing garments. Sashes, belts, edging on necklines and sleeve ends, bindings on lapels, pocket squares, neckwear, and hat trims can be made from small amounts of fabric in a color that visually pulls the costumes together. More on how to use existing garments and materials will be discussed in Chapter 10.

2
WORKING WITH THE DESIGN TEAM TO DEVELOP THE COLOR SCHEME

Costumes do not exist in a vacuum; their colors are seen in visual dialogue with the work of the other stage designers and the director. Even a beautifully colored group of costumes will be pointless if they do not work harmoniously and intelligently with the other visual elements. Every play is a unique world created from specific costumes, lights, projections, sets, and directorial choices, in a venue of a specific size. The more a costume designer understands the other areas of design, the better prepared they can be to make optimal choices that work within a particular production. By working well with the other designers and the director of a production, a smart costume designer can create a color scheme that is an integral component of the play.

Scenery

The set provides the background for the costumes. Depending on the design schedule of a specific theatre company, the set and costumes may be developed at the same time, or the set may be designed and the colors chosen prior to the costume designer even starting their design process. In other cases, the set may be rented from another company, and the colors will need to be ascertained from (hopefully accurate) photos because the colors will not be alterable.

The size and configuration of the venue will affect how the audience will perceive costumes. Depending on the configuration of the theatre itself, the proscenium, side stages, backstage space, the back wall, the grand drape, or masking curtains may be major color factors on stage and will affect the level of contrast that will be needed for the costumes to be visible. Consider all the areas of color that are contained within the setting. Scenic interiors may have wall colors and patterns, trim, floor treatments, and draperies that the actors will be standing near. Scenery depicting outdoor spaces will tend to have large Blue sky areas, with Green grass, Brown dirt or wood-tone floors, Green foliage, and Grey stone buildings or garden walls. These items may be painted in realistic colors, more-than-natural intensified colors, or in Sepia tones. For a play that is actually presented outdoors, a background of real nature and the sky may be the main scenic elements. For arena theatres, the colors of the seats and the audience's clothing will end up being much of the distant background. For a minimalist production, black curtains or the theatre's backstage walls may be the default background. For a production that uses many projections, the pale projection surfaces may dominate the stage. For a musical, there may be a number of sets in different colors for various scenes and production numbers, along with masking for in-one scenes.

If the play depicts the outdoors but is presented inside a theatre, assume that a large Blue area will be part of the scenic picture. Even if Blue is your desired color for the main character, and Blue would be the perfect color for the period, if the set is going to be Blue, there will need to be some discussion between the designers and the director. This may be a matter of adjusting the set color to a Greyed light Blue and the costumes to a deeper or brighter Blue-Green. Or, it may be a situation where a completely different color is the best choice for a particular costume. In any case, potential color conflicts should be anticipated and discussed cordially to find the best overall solution for the production. Even if the director and/or design team have agreed on a color scheme or inspiration in advance, each designer may have very different interpretations of how to use the chosen colors, which should be worked out well before any concrete steps are taken to purchase the fabric or paint the walls.

Gather as much accurate information as you can about the set colors as soon as possible in the design process in order the make the best costume color choices. All of the set color choices will make a major impact on the color choices a costume designer can make. Remember, the set is a much larger area of the theatrical space than the costumed actors, even for crowd scenes in opera. Against that large volume of space, actors can be lost. This may be owing to actors and the set being in the same colors, or because the set is brighter and bolder than the costume colors. In either situation, garments that appear realistic and interesting in the fitting room can appear dull and uninteresting on stage.

In addition to the theatre itself and the scenic needs of the script, the set designer may have particular colors that they gravitate towards, such as Blue or Grey or Brown, that are likely to be part of their designs. If you know the scenic designer's work or can research their past productions, you may find that they have a group of colors that they use regularly. Keep this information in the back of your mind as you develop the costume colors and keep checking back on the scenic colors during the set painting process if possible.

If the designers are working remotely from one another, timely communication is even more vital. Ideally, each member of the team should scan their color choices and send them electronically or upload them to a shared file so that everyone else can see where each designer is heading. Then, **actually mail or distribute samples** of color paint chips and fabric swatches to the rest of the team. Even then, remember that a small fabric swatch, paint chip, or image on a computer is not always indicative of the colors that will ultimately appear on stage. A small paint chip may appear much brighter on a large wall area, or the colors may be mixed to a higher level of saturation when it is time to paint. Looking at fabric swatches, even ⅛-yard samples, is not the same as seeing the entire costume with the actor wearing it. However, whether the design team is in the same room or working separately, early and accurate communication can head off the worst color clashes or too-close matches that might otherwise occur. Full-color renderings for the sets and costumes are vital for getting a fuller sense of what will end up onstage, and uploading these to a shared file or distributing physical color copies will help each designer reference what the other designers are doing.

My advice to theatre costume designers is this: **you are not designing a realistic movie. Make the colors stronger than you would in real life so that the actors can stand out from the scenery. The scenery is larger than the costumed actors and will always impact how the costumes are perceived.**

Lighting

The lighting design tends to be developed after the set and costumes have been designed. However, this doesn't mean that the lighting designer is only reacting to these two design areas and trying to make them look as lovely as possible. Lighting designers illuminate the stage, but they also help set the mood of the production and scenes, underline specific moments, indicate time of day and season, draw attention to important characters and actions, and create texture and pattern through gobos and instrument choices. Some lighting designers favor non-realistic uses of color inspired by rock shows, whereas others favor strongly shaded effects inspired by dance lighting.

Light is color and color is light. The lighting designer's work has a huge impact on how costume colors appear onstage. During a production meeting, the lighting designer may discuss moods for various scenes, may show photos as color research, or may distribute colored gel swatches to show their color direction. In some situations, the lighting designer may set up some of their intended instruments and colors on the stage in front of a wall painted in the intended set colors and with bolts of the intended costume fabric colors. However, remember that, in all of these cases, the **lighting indicated will not be exactly what will be seen on the finished stage**. This may be owing to the size of the venue in which the production will be staged, which will affect the amount of light that needs to be shone onstage for actors to be visible to the audience. Some of this is owing to the physical instruments that the lighting designer will be using, some of this is owing to the combination of instruments and directions of the lights, and some of this is owing to director input once they see lights on the actors during dress rehearsals.

Instruments

Colored gels in front of incandescent lighting instruments can create a spectrum of different colors on the stage while also dulling down colors that do not contain the gel color. In addition, unless the instrument is programmed to work at 100% intensity and is reasonably new, there will be an amber/orange shift to the light that is shone onstage by that instrument. The light color emitted from incandescent instruments will have a warm effect, which may be hard on subtle patterns or cool costume colors.

Modern, programmable LED instruments allow for quicker shifts of colors within a show and more ability to fine-tune colors during dress rehearsals. However, not all theatres have these instruments, or they may only have a small number of them. And, the later in the process that a costume designer makes a color change request, the less likely that the lighting designer can make a change, no matter how seemingly simple the request may be if they are using LED instruments. After all, as with all of us, the lighting designer likely already has a long list of adjustments to make between each dress rehearsal. As the range of colors available from LEDs is large, lighting designers may opt for more intense colors than they would choose in gel form. The light from LED instruments (as of this writing) tends to be clear and sharp, therefore appearing cool compared with classic incandescent instruments. Costume colors will appear to have sharper contrasts under LEDs than the more blended tones of colors under incandescent lights.

Spotlights are used more often for musicals, operas, and concerts than for intimate dramas. They help draw attention to the main characters and underscore important moments. Owing to the intensity of spotlights, they can also visually flatten the details and fade the colors of the costumes.

Fluorescent fixtures are not used onstage as much as the instrument types discussed above. However, theatre work lights, often fluorescent, may be used for a less-idealized effect in some scenes. Fluorescent lights will dull down colors and make them appear drabber than they actually are because the light tends to have a Blue or Green cast to it. This type of instrument will show harsh contrasts of fabric colors and makeup and flatten out costume details.

A group of instruments can project different colors that combine to make a white light effect that is more interesting than that of un-gelled instruments and create sheer colors that show in the folds of the costume. As lighting colors will dull those fabric colors that do not contain the colors of the light, a grouping of different-colored light beams in combination will flatter a wider range of colors in costumes and scenery than a single-colored light beam. At the same time, be thoughtful when selecting subtle color combinations or "shot" or "changeable" (i.e., cross-dyed) fabrics, as they may not appear as planned when viewed under stage lights.

Using Gobos, or cut-out pieces of metal or other material held in front of the lighting instruments, results in a light beam that has a pattern, image, or texture. It may project the image of window light, clouds, snow, leaves, or a more abstract, broken-up pattern that adds interest to the stage picture. Gobos reduce the amount of light transmitted to the stage, affecting how costume colors and garment shapes appear to the audience.

Direction of Light

Light in nature often comes from above, but theatre light can come from the sides, the back, the front, straight down, at an angle from above, and up from the stage floor. Ideally, the variety of lighting angles will give an overall rounded effect that will show off the textures and volume of the garments. The angles of the light falling on an actor will not necessarily alter the costume colors, but the effect of lighting angles is worth mentioning. For more technical discussion of lighting, see Appendix 3.

It is important to learn to speak the language of lighting in order to work as a team with the lighting designer. As the set is the largest stage design element, it often happens that a lighting designer will concentrate on enhancing the set with light. Lighting designers tend to focus their instruments and determine the transmission levels on a set without actors, so that the result may be a lighting design that flatters the set rather than the costumes. Despite using an assistant to walk the stage during the focus process in order to check for gaps in overall lighting coverage, flattering costume colors and actor skin tones may not necessarily be foremost in the lighting designer's mind.

Lighting will make or break how the costumes look. Be sure to give the lighting designer as much concrete color and texture information as possible with fabric samples, color copies of renderings, and photos of garment fittings and by inviting them to the costume shop to see the costumes in process. Just as strong highlights and shadows are used in stage makeup, clear color contrasts in the costumes are necessary so that they can be clearly seen on stage. In order to "punch through" the slight haze that colored light creates on stage, **use strong contrasts and clear details so that they are visible to the audience. At the same time, avoid very high contrasts such as black and white costumes if you can**, or at least tone down the bright whites. Very high contrasts are difficult for the lighting designer to flatter equally at both ends of the contrast scale.

Projections

Projections are increasingly important to stage productions. They can comment on a scene, illustrate a character's inner life, add a cinematic aspect to a play, act as scenery, and augment lighting.

As projections consist of light, color, and movement, they will impact costume colors. During a production meeting, it is important to get a sense of how the projections will be used, where the projection surface(s) will be located, the placement of the projectors(s), whether projections will fall on the costumes, how close the actors will be to the projection surfaces, and the desired overall effects.

A projection surface will draw the audience's focus, particularly if the images move or there is text included. If the actors are not adjacent to the projection surface, strong costume colors and shapes can counteract the distraction. On the other hand, if the actors are used as a projection surface, they may need to be dressed in non-patterned pale colors and simple garments so that the projections are more visible. If the projectors are positioned in front of the stage, actors may become unwitting projection surfaces at some point if they move too near the screens. Rear screen projectors are best used with a deep backstage area so that the actors have the room to cross backstage during the projection sequences without walking between the projector and the screen. However, a major benefit of rear-screen projections is that the actors never become unwitting projection screens.

Sound

Sound design does not specifically affect costume color, but it is worth mentioning those aspects of sound that need to be factored into the costume design. If actors are wearing microphones, the mics may either hook over one ear or be worn in the center of the forehead. Wires will need to be hidden under a wig or within the actor's hair and will be taped up the back of the wearer's neck. The battery pack is approximately the size of a deck of cards and will need to be secured at some place on the body. Costume fittings should be done while the actor is wearing something that represents the battery pack, in order to avoid problems during first dress rehearsal. In addition, the actors will need to have the mics put on them by a sound technician or a dresser, prior to getting fully into costume for each performance.

The Director

The director's sense of color will have a major impact on the colors chosen for costumes. By choosing a specific play, setting it in a particular time period, and emphasizing an approach to the play, the director's input has a huge effect on selecting the colors that will be right for a production.

Try to ask for the director's production color ideas as soon as you can. As people have personal associations and preferences for colors, find out **why** the colors seem right to the director. It is especially helpful to find out which colors **do not** work, so that you can eliminate them from consideration. Some directors start the first production meeting with images that have inspired them. In this situation, it is helpful to find out how the director envisions the images they present as being worked into the eventual design scheme.

At the same time, if you have a strong color impression, share this with the director. Show actual color pictures rather than using color terms such as "Happy" or "Autumnal." Different people have different senses of what these terms might mean, and it is clearer if there are actual color samples to discuss. If you have color ideas that differ from the director's, you still may be able to use them if you use the colors thoughtfully. In fact, the director's initial images may not ultimately be what they actually want, but a result of their feeling that they should have **some** type of image for the first design meeting. Examples of color schemes are discussed in Chapters 3–7 and may be a starting point towards communicating with a director.

Sometimes, it is helpful to show a specific color combination or group of large fabric samples to a director during a working design meeting in order to illustrate how the colors you are considering would be perfect for the production at hand. If the director likes to get their hands on materials, a costume designer can show them options of fabrics draped over dress forms, demonstrate options of how to combine the colors, and encourage the director to help move colors around until both of you are pleased with the result. However, some directors may not necessarily be comfortable working with color and fabrics and are happy to let designers take the lead in this area. In that case, be sure to discuss, and show, the color scheme to the scenic, lighting, and projection designers during production meetings so that all design areas are aware of each other's palettes.

There are times when a director has specific responses to color that are highly personal. Some directors have negative associates with women in Red and, therefore, will not allow a Red costume on the leading lady. Another director may object to the traditional Pink color for a character, because they were forced to wear Pink as a child. Yet another may associate a color with a parent or former partner and not be able to see the color in the context of the production. These objections can be hard to surmount, and it may be advisable to avoid using the objectionable colors. In the examples above, a Red dress was changed to a deep Cool Rose dress, and bright Pink garments were replaced with a variety of clear colors in graphic patterns because of the directors' dislike of the original color choices.

If you suggest a color that the director does not like, be prepared to explain and defend your choice, and to have the choice rejected. On the other hand, it is also possible to propose colors that a director was not sure of during the initial discussions. The point is that there will be give and take with any color decisions, and **the sooner a designer can show what they are thinking of and why the choices work for the production, the better.**

A good costume designer can take a director to a place they didn't know they really wanted to go with color. To do this, the designer needs to:

1. Actively listen to what the director is saying.
2. Be very familiar with the script through repeated readings and research about the play's background.
3. Have a strong understanding of clothing from the time and place in which the play is set.
4. Be sensitive to the beauty of each actor.
5. Be willing to learn and be challenged during the design process.
6. Be practical and able to stick to a schedule and budget.
7. And trust that the director knows what they are doing.

Through your understanding of these points, a director will see that **you** know what you are doing and will be open to your ideas.

If the director has cultural associations with colors that differ from yours, or the script is based in a culture or period different from your own, it is time to do some research into the different meanings of color. With the caveat that color meanings may shift over time, a chart of color associations is presented in Appendix 1, and a list of period color preferences is contained in Appendix 2.

Of course, each costume designer will have their own sense of color, as will each director, actor, and set, lighting, and projection designer. A successful color scheme will need to take ALL these color preferences into consideration, along with the color decisions that are suggested by the time period or mood of the production. Some costume designers may love to use Red, whereas a director may be uncomfortable having a character in Red onstage, and an actor may have coloring that would look bad in a Red costume or may just dislike wearing Red. The set design may feature a large Red-toned background that needs to be considered and negotiated over. The lighting designer may use a Red or Amber gel in particular scenes, which will strongly affect how costume colors are perceived. The projection designer may plan Red images in order to set a mood, but the Red may overwhelm the costume colors. All of these are factors to be considered when choosing garments, fabrics, and colors.

3

COLOR THEORY AND COLOR MIXING

Before exploring how to combine colors, it is useful to understand the components of an individual color. This chapter covers color terminology and aspects of mixing hues to arrive at specific colors. Colors can be defined by specific terminology, as follows.

Hue

The **Hue** is the name of the color, such as Red or Green, as it exists on the color wheel. This is the full-Intensity/Saturation version of a color.

Value

The **Value** refers to the quality of **lightness or darkness** of a hue. This entails both the **inherent lightness** of the hue itself at full Intensity, such as Yellow (which is considered high-value) or Blue (which is considered low-value), and the **adjusted Value** made by adding White or Black to a hue. Values of a particular hue will range from a high-value Tint, made by adding White to the hue, to a low-value Shade, made by adding Black to the hue.

FIGURE 3.1 Red and Green hues at full Saturation

FIGURE 3.2 Yellow is inherently high-Value, whereas Blue is inherently lower Value than the Yellow, even when both hues are at full Saturation

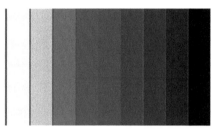

FIGURE 3.3 Blue adjusted from a high-Value Tint to a low-Value Shade; 25% increases in White or Black were made at each step from the central saturated Blue, outwards to White and Black

Intensity/Saturation

The **Intensity** or **Saturation** is the Purity of the hue, ranging from very pure and bright at full Intensity and moving towards Neutralized or Subdued by being mixed with another hue.

Mixing a hue with its opposite on the color wheel, known as its Complement, is considered to be **Neutralizing** the hue, because the mix with the Complement will most emphatically diminish the Intensity of the original hue. However, if you are adding the Complement to a hue with paints, the result will be different than when adding the Complement with a computer owing to the different ways that colors mix in different mediums.

FIGURE 3.4 Red neutralized on a computer by reducing the amount of Red by 25% in each step

FIGURE 3.5 Red neutralized on a computer by reducing the amount of Red **plus** reducing Saturation by 25% in each step

FIGURE 3.6 Red neutralized on a computer by adding its (pigment) complement, Green, 25% in each step. The result turns Yellow, as Red plus Green creates Yellow when mixing the **lighting primaries**

FIGURE 3.7 Color range from Scarlet Red to Emerald Green in watercolor paint, neutralized by increasing the amount of Emerald Green paint added to the original Scarlet in each step

FIGURE 3.8 Color range from Orange to Blue, with Neutralized steps along the way. On a computer, the Red was reduced by 20% at the same time the Blue was increased by 20% at each step

Any time one hue is mixed with another hue, the Intensity of the original hue is diminished in some manner. In this book, a color that is mixed with its Complement will be referred to as having been **Neutralized**, a color that is mixed with Grey will be referred to as a **Tone** of the original color, and a color that is mixed with any other color in order to lessen its Intensity will be referred to as having been **Subdued**.

FIGURE 3.9   Yellow, with Grey added on a computer to create a **Tone** by reducing the contrast by 20% in each step until a deep Ochre Gold is created. After that point, the final two colors on the right side of this array had their contrast reduced by 10% instead of 20% because they quickly became Grey

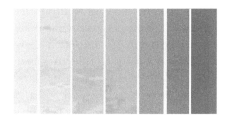

FIGURE 3.10   Yellow, with Green added to **Subdue** the range of Toned hues in Figure 3.9. On a computer, this was achieved by reducing the amount of Red in the mix as an overall wash over Figure 3.9. This further Subdued the colors that had been previously Toned with Grey (contrast reduced on the computer) to make interesting colors with less intensity than the original Yellow hue. The resulting colors have a slight Green aspect

FIGURE 3.11   Yellow, with Green added to **Subdue** the Yellow. On a computer, this was created by reducing the Red in the mix by 20% in each step. The resulting colors have a definite Green aspect

FIGURE 3.12 Neutral colors

A color such as White, Grey, Beige, Tan, Brown, or Black that blends well with a wide variety of other colors is referred to as a **Neutral color**.

To add verbal complexity to this situation, in popular discussion, the Neutral colors just described are sometimes referred to as a Monochromatic Color scheme. However, **in this book, Monochromatic** will be used to discuss a color scheme based on **one hue, with or without the addition of Neutrals and** *whether or not* **the hue has had its Value or Intensity altered or has been Neutralized or Subdued**.

Further, when discussing color in more technical terms, there can be some confusion between colors that are popularly considered to be **Neutrals** and colors that have been **Neutralized** or **Subdued**. For the purposes of this book, a **Neutralized** color is one that has been **mixed from its Saturated form by the addition of its Complementary color** – it has been reduced from its full intensity by the addition of some of the opposite color on the color wheel. Therefore, the Intensity or Saturation of Neutralized colors is **lower** than that of the original hue. For example, Brown is considered a "Neutral" color because it works well in composition with a variety of hues. However, Brown is created in part by **neutralizing** Orange with its Complement, Blue, and **then** by adjusting the color through adding Shading with Black, Toning with Grey, and Subduing it with some Green or some Red, depending on the desired result.

During the process of paint mixing or developing a dye color, **hues other than the Complement** *can also* **be added** to the starting hue in order to adjust the color towards the desired lower-intensity result. In this book, these mixes will be referred to as **Subdued** colors. For example, a version of Brown is theoretically mixed when Orange is neutralized with its Complement, Blue. However, depending on whether the Brown that an artist is trying to create is Warm or Cool, and the exact Intensity, Value, and Temperature of the original Orange and Blue hues used in the mix, the resulting color may or may not be what was desired, as in Figure 3.13. In that case, a mixed Brown can also be **Subdued** by the addition of Red, Yellow, or Green, depending on the particular Brown that is desired. A Subdued color has been **blended away from its original pure state towards being a much more complex and less Saturated or Intense color, but is not exclusively mixed from a hue and its Complement**.

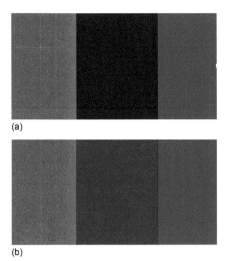

(a)

(b)

FIGURE 3.13   (a) Orange pigment neutralized with Blue will actually yield a Plum-Brown-Grey color rather than the expected Grey. (b) However, starting with certain paint or dye colors, the blended result will actually have a Green tinge to it, as seen here. Neither is a real Brown, although either might be useful in some instances

FIGURE 3.14   Grey, Green, Black, and Red were added to the Plum-Brown color in the center register of Figure 3.13a to create a recognizable Brown color

The Color Wheel

The color wheel is a schematic layout of 12 hues in a prism or rainbow, pulled into a ring that shows the colors blending from one to another:

The 12-hue color wheel will be used as the organizing principle for this book, starting and ending with Red. Purple, which is technically called Violet, will be referred to hereafter as Purple because it is the more commonly used name for this specific hue. However, variants of Violet will be referred to as Red-Violet and Blue-Violet.

TABLE 3.1 The Color Wheel

		Red		
	Red-Orange		Red-Violet	
Orange				Purple (Violet)
Yellow-Orange		*Center Point*		Blue-Violet
Yellow				Blue
	Yellow-Green		Blue-Green	
		Green		

FIGURE 3.15 Spectrum of hues

Primary Colors

Primary colors are the three-to-four irreducible hues that are mixed to create other colors. Pigments and Lighting colors use three Primaries, whereas Printing colors use four.

Pigments

For Pigments such as paint or dye, Red, Yellow, and Blue are considered the Primary colors. By combining two Primary colors, the Secondary colors of Orange (Red plus Yellow), Green (Yellow plus Blue), and Purple (Blue plus Red) are created. By combining a Primary with a Secondary color, the Tertiary colors of Red-Orange, Yellow-Orange, Yellow-Green, Blue-Green, Blue-Violet, and Red-Violet are created. Mixing multiple Tertiary or Secondary colors will yield increasingly complex and Subdued hues as the combinations move further away from the original Primary colors.

Pigment colors utilize what is known as Subtractive color mixing, because **combining colors reduces** the purity of each hue and results in an increasingly Subdued color. Each component pigment absorbs light wavelengths, and so the result is a complex mixed color in which **the only hues reflected are those light wavelengths that the pigments do not absorb**. The more pigments that are mixed together in a color, the more wavelengths are absorbed, and the more Subdued the resulting color. According to Subtractive color theory, mixing all three Primary pigment colors together should create Black, although, in actual practice, the resulting color often tends to be a Subdued Grey-Purple-Brown because of impurities in the Primary pigments themselves. For painting and dyeing, a Warm set and a Cool set of hues are helpful to have on hand when mixing colors, because the texture of and impurities in the paint or dye itself will reduce the ability of colors to mix completely.

Light

For Light, whether generated from lighting instruments or on a computer screen, the Primary colors are Red, Green, and Blue, which may be combined to create the Secondary colors of Yellow (Red plus Green), Magenta (Red plus Blue), and Cyan (Blue plus Green).

Lighting colors utilize what is known as Additive color mixing, because lighting wavelengths **reveal** colors. The color on an object is only revealed to the extent that the **color is contained in the light shone onto the object**. Think of the effect of dull greyness that one sees before turning on a lamp on dark mornings: color in objects is seen owing to the light that illuminates the object. According to Additive color theory, mixing all three Primary lighting colors together will create White light, although, in practice, the light produced is also affected by the power with which the instrument is run, the age of the instrument or computer monitor, and the type of lamp used to create illumination. Because of the additive nature of lighting, many lighting designers use instruments with a mix of colored gels in order to create more interesting and dynamic lighting that appears to be White but shows a variety of colors in garment folds.

Printing

For Printing, such as book reproductions or color copies of artwork, the Primary colors are Magenta (Blue-Red), Cyan (Blue-Green), Yellow, and Black. As printing Primaries are different than lighting Primaries or pigment Primaries, it is most helpful to have actual swatches of fabric when matching colors and choosing materials. When moving between printed reproductions based on Printing Primaries, computer displays based on Lighting Primaries, and paint or dye colors based on Pigment Primaries, be prepared for some unexpected alterations in the color that you are trying to create, because **each group of colors is a translation of the others, even if the hue names are the same**.

The color samples in this book are derived from a variety of sources. The intent of the book is the service of art, not science; the color samples are included to clarify points of discussion, not as scientifically measurable hues. You will also see the result of the translation process in this book's images as discussed above. Many of the color samples were taken from one source and then manipulated to get a desired result – the original colors were painted or printed with pigments, then scanned into a computer and adjusted, and then converted to printing primary colors for publication. Therefore, the color samples presented here are not perfect ideals of particular hues, and the method of arriving at a particular color may not be as important as the color itself, especially as seen in combination with other colors. Where it adds to the reader's understanding of what they are seeing, the different ways in which the resulting colors were arrived at will be noted. In other cases, the exact recipe for a particular color is not as important as the color itself, as seen on the printed book page.

Mixing Hues to Create Colors

As a designer gets more practice looking at different colors and different **versions** of colors, they will start to be able to isolate some of the component hues within a color. For example, there is a reason that a typical set of paints or dyes does not only consist of three Primary colors plus Black. Instead, there is often a Scarlet (warm) Red and a Crimson (medium to cool) Red; a Golden (warm) and Lemon (cool) Yellow; a Chrome (warm), Viridian (medium cool) and an Emerald (low value cool) Green; a Cerulean (warm), Cobalt, and Prussian (low value cool) Blue, as well as other hues plus Neutrals to allow a painter to create a full range of colors.

For example, mixing a cool Red and a cool Yellow will yield a different Orange than mixing a warm Red and a medium Yellow, which are both different than Orange right from the paint tube. All of the resulting Oranges will be valuable in the right situation. Further, the Orange that is mixed from two other hues will often look less Saturated than the Orange paint from the paint tube. To some designers, the mixed color looks less Saturated because the two component hues contain some trace hues that subdue one other, but other designers may disagree. Let your own eyes be your guide, as long as you have concrete examples of your intended colors to show your collaborators when you are discussing a theoretical color scheme.

FIGURE 3.16 Orange watercolor

FIGURE 3.17 Orange from a scanned paint sample, manipulated to full intensity on the computer

FIGURE 3.18 Orange mixed from 50% Vermillion Red, 50% Lemon Yellow

FIGURE 3.19 Orange mixed from 50% Vermillion Red, 50% Yellow Medium

FIGURE 3.20 Orange mixed from 50% Crimson, 50% Lemon Yellow

FIGURE 3.21 Orange mixed from 50% Crimson, 50% Yellow Medium

FIGURE 3.22 Orange mixed from 50% Scarlet, 50% Lemon Yellow

FIGURE 3.23 Orange mixed from 50% Scarlet, 50% Yellow Medium

FIGURE 3.24 Orange created on a computer from Red with Yellow added. On the computer, adding 50% Yellow was achieved by increasing Green and Red colors, as Red and Green create Yellow in lighting

It is a great learning experience to compare the results created when mixing different versions and amounts of colors to arrive at a desired result. The most important outcome of such an exercise is to help a designer to see colors and their nuances more fully. Experiment with changing Values, altering Intensities, and adjusting Hues in order to see how different colors are created. Once you get comfortable with the different aspects of a single color – Hue, Intensity/Saturation, and Value – and how to mix different hues, it is time to combine different colors into compositions.

4

COLOR HARMONY

As with the characters in a play, colors are most often used in combinations rather than existing in isolation. A **Color Harmony** is a combination of hues, based on their placements on the color wheel. Color harmonies can be bold or subtle. They can be a starting point for establishing a color scheme or a way to organize an existing group of costumes and fabrics into a coherent whole. Based on the number of hues that are in combination, the colors can help illustrate character dynamics.

One-Hue Color Harmonies

Monochromatic or One-Color schemes are based on a single hue used through-out the composition. They will create a sense of unity and/or stylization. For a one-color scheme, be sure that variations on the hue, garment shape, or texture differences are clear to the audience, in order to avoid a boring effect.

Monochromatic approaches may be further distinguished as follows:

True Monochromatic

This is one hue of a single Value (often the Medium, high-Intensity hue that is on the color wheel) with no accent colors, Tints and Shades of the hue, or Neutrals added to the composition. In this case, the shapes and/or textures of the costumes will need to be clearly differentiated because color variations do not help identify characters. This is a particularly stylized color approach and is rarely used, except for an "all-White" costume design – which is often actually made up of a range of very light neutrals.

Variations on this theme include:

- One hue of a specific value, with **Black and/or White** as a large aspect of the overall look.

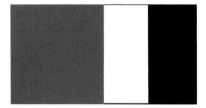

FIGURE 4.1   Blue with Black and White

- One hue of a specific value, with Black **and** White and using **stripes and other surface patterns** to add interest.

FIGURE 4.2   Blue variations with patterns

Broad Monochromatic

Broad Monochromatic color schemes are based on tints, shades, and tones of a single hue. In terms of color theory, a Tint is a hue mixed with White, a Shade is a hue mixed with Black, and a Tone is a hue mixed with Grey. For those who are uncertain about combining colors, using different Light, Dark, and/or Greyed versions of a single hue is a good way to create visual harmony. Be sure to choose fabrics in a variety of Textures to create visual interest. Figures 4.3–4.8 show tints and shades for Primary and Secondary hues.

Variations on Broad Monochromatic color schemes include:

- One hue, with Tints and Shades of that hue. Black and White, **or** a Neutral light and dark shade such as Cream and Brown, are added as a large part of the overall look.
- One hue, with Tints and Shades of that hue, **plus** a variety of Neutral Whites, Beiges, Greys, Browns, and Blacks
- Light to Dark versions of one hue on one character vs. Dark to Light on others, using the same monochromatic scheme but placing the colors differently on the body.

FIGURE 4.3 Red, Pink, Burgundy (added Black and Grey for Shade)

FIGURE 4.4 Orange, Peach, Rust (added Black and Grey for Shade)

FIGURE 4.5 Yellow, Ecru, Gold (added Black and Grey for Shade)

FIGURE 4.6 Green, Mint, Forest (added Black and Grey for Shade)

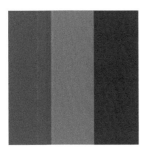

FIGURE 4.7 Blue, pale Blue, Royal (added Black and Grey for Shade)

FIGURE 4.8 Purple, Lavender, Eggplant (added Black and Grey for Shade)

FIGURE 4.9 Red, Pink, Burgundy, White, and Black

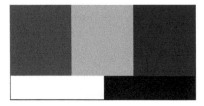

FIGURE 4.10 Red, Pink, Burgundy, Cream, and Brown

FIGURE 4.11 Red, Pink, Burgundy, White, Grey, Beige, Tan, Brown, and Black

See Figures 4.12–4.13.

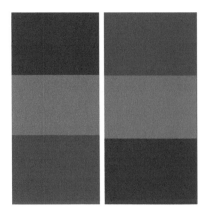

FIGURE 4.12 Blue values arranged in opposing "stacks"

FIGURE 4.13 Using pale tints of Yellow and Yellow-Orange to create opposing "stacks" of color on costumes

Tint-and-Shade Monochromatic

Very harmonious monochromatic color groupings involve a Tint and a Tone and/or a Shade of a hue, **avoiding the pure hue** except for accents. In the list below, I am including the common color names that refer to the Tints and Shades of a hue. Examples are shown in Figures 4.14–4.19:

FIGURE 4.14 Pink and Burgundy (added Black and Grey)

FIGURE 4.15 Peach and Rust (added Black and Grey)

FIGURE 4.16 Ecru and Gold (added Black and Grey)

FIGURE 4.17 Mint and Forest (added Black and Grey)

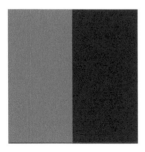

FIGURE 4.18 Pale Blue and Royal (added Black and Grey)

FIGURE 4.19   Lavender and Eggplant (added Black and Grey)

Neutrals (and Neutralized or Subdued Colors)

Many monochromatic schemes are based on Neutrals, with or without a more definite Hue in the combinations.

Neutrals are discussed in Chapter 3, but they bear examining more than once. The popular definition of a "Neutral color" tends to be a **low-Intensity color that can be combined attractively with many other hues because the Neutral color has lower intensity than the other hues in the combination.** This is the definition of "Neutral" that this book will follow. A Neutral color can seem almost like a "non-color" and works well as a background hue. Using Tints and Shades of Neutral Greys, Blacks, Browns, Beiges, and Whites, without other saturated hues, is referred to as a "Neutral Color Approach."

Examples of Neutral color combinations are shown in Figures 4.20 and 4.21.

Neutralized and **Subdued** colors have been blended with another hue, whether with the hue's complement for a Neutralized color or another color (or colors) for a Subdued color. They tend to blend well with one another, because they often contain so many trace hues that they are somehow related to one another. Combinations of Neutralized and Subdued colors include those shown in Figures 4.22 and 4.23.

 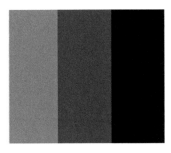

FIGURE 4.20   Grey, White, Medium Grey, Charcoal, and Black – all are variations of White-to-Black

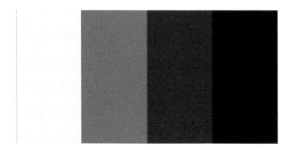

FIGURE 4.21 Beige, Tan, Brown, and Dark Brown – all are variations of Beige-to-Brown

FIGURE 4.22 Dark Warm Grey, Greyed Brown, and Grey – all are variations of Grey

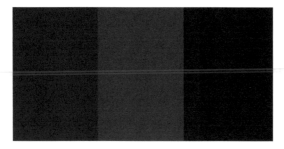

FIGURE 4.23 Dark Greyed Navy, Slate Blue-Grey, and Blue-Black – all are variations of Blue

Neutrals, Neutralized Colors, and Subdued Colors with Accents

To add interest to less-intense color schemes, use a striking **Accent** color where you want to draw focus in a smaller area. Taupes, Beiges, and Greys run the risk of appearing dull. Add a single deep color such as dark Red, Rust, Olive Green, Grey-Blue, Blue-Purple, or Ochre to give a richer effect to an otherwise subtle color scheme. Add an Intense color, such as pure Red, Green, or Blue for a bold effect. A variety of possible accent colors to choose from are pictured: examples of these color combinations are shown in Figures 4.24–4.27.

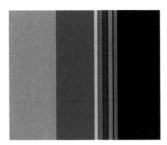

FIGURE 4.24   Grey, White, Medium Grey, Charcoal, and Black plus: Ochre, Blue, Burgundy, Olive Green, or Red

FIGURE 4.25   Beige, Tan, Brown, and Dark Brown plus: Rusty Red, Warm Red, or Blue-Violet

FIGURE 4.26   Taupe, Greyed Brown, and Grey plus: Red-Violet, Red, Rust, Orange, or Deep Green

FIGURE 4.27   Dark Greyed Navy, Slate Blue-Grey, and Blue-Black plus: Pink, Red, Deep Green, Purple, Olive Green, or Blue

Bi-Chromatic Harmonies

Bi-chromatic or Two-Color schemes use two main hues. This may create either opposition or unity, depending on how the hues are used in the composition. These approaches may be further distinguished as follows:

Complementary Color Harmony

Two hues can be used to create oppositions between two characters or character groups. Complementary hues lie opposite to one another on the color wheel and thus have the greatest contrast possible. Two opposite-position pure hues placed next to one another in equal proportions can appear to visually vibrate because the colors have no component hues that they share, and so they visually "fight" one another.

True Complementary Colors

True Complementary color schemes feature hues that are **opposite** one another through the center point of the color wheel. Refer to Table 3.1 for the Color Wheel. Not all possible color combinations are pictured below:

FIGURE 4.28   Red vs. Green

FIGURE 4.29   Orange vs. Blue

FIGURE 4.30   Yellow vs. Purple

FIGURE 4.31   Red-Violet vs. Yellow-Green

FIGURE 4.32   Blue-Green vs. Red-Orange

FIGURE 4.33   Blue-Violet vs. Yellow-Orange

These color combinations work well for **oppositions** or for making a strong statement. On stage, a Complementary color scheme can illustrate two opposing armies, warring families, or other strong divisions. In real life, these combinations are often used for sports team jerseys because they draw attention on the field. They may also be used for holiday colors or for children's products.

Unequal Complements

For most non-oppositional uses, try to avoid an equal balance between two strong, contrasting hues. Two hues of similar visual weight can be distributed equally among a group of costumes. However, the colors will usually **not be used in equal amounts** within an individual costume. More exploration of using unequal amounts of colors in a color scheme is contained in Chapter 5.

Unequal Complements Using Adjusted Values, Neutralized Colors, and Subdued Colors

For more a harmonious composition based on two colors, lower the Value, reduce the Intensity, Neutralize or Subdue **one** of the colors, or use the colors in **different**

sizes. It is more harmonious to mix Complementary colors if **one** of the colors is chosen as the Dominant color and comprises approximately 60–66% of the combination. Use the other color in the complementary pair as a Supporting color in the smaller area of the composition. Depending on the desired result, one may use either a pure or adjusted version of the hue in either the larger or smaller color area.

If you wish to create a Tint of a hue, mix with White. If you wish to darken or create a Shade of a hue, mix with Black. If you wish to create a Tone, mix with Grey. If you wish to Neutralize a hue, mix with its Complement. If you wish to Subdue the hue, mix with another color depending on the desired end result.

Not all possible combinations are shown in the samples below, but notes have been added as to how the less-intense colors were arrived at. More exploration of using unequal amounts of colors in a color scheme is contained in Chapter 5. Variations on this idea include:

- Complementary harmonies, with reduced-Intensity hues **as the larger area**: see Figures 4.34–4.39.

FIGURE 4.34   Burgundy (Black added to Red) and Green

FIGURE 4.35   Rust (Black added to Orange) and Blue

FIGURE 4.36   Golden Ochre (Black added to Yellow) and Purple

FIGURE 4.37   Forest Green (Black added to Green) and Red

FIGURE 4.38   Navy (Black added to Blue) and Orange

FIGURE 4.39   Eggplant (Black added to Purple) and Yellow

- Complementary harmonies, with reduced-Intensity hues **in both areas**: see Figures 4.40–4.45.

FIGURE 4.40   Burgundy and Forest Green

FIGURE 4.41   Rust and Navy Blue

FIGURE 4.42 Golden Ochre and Eggplant

FIGURE 4.43 Forest Green and Burgundy

FIGURE 4.44 Navy and Rust

FIGURE 4.45 Eggplant and Golden Ochre

- Complementary harmonies, with reduced-Intensity hues as **the smaller area**: see Figures 4.46–4.51.

FIGURE 4.46 Red and Forest Green

FIGURE 4.47   Orange and Navy

FIGURE 4.48   Yellow and Eggplant

FIGURE 4.49   Green and Burgundy

FIGURE 4.50   Blue and Rust

FIGURE 4.51   Purple and Golden Ochre

Partial Triads

Two of the three hues in a Triad combination can be used in a composition, ignoring the implied third color. More discussion of Triad color combinations will be discussed in the section on Tri-Chromatic color harmonies, later in this chapter. These combinations include:

• Primary Partial Triads: see Figures 4.52–4.54.

FIGURE 4.52 Red and Yellow

FIGURE 4.53 Yellow and Blue

FIGURE 4.54 Blue and Red

• Secondary Partial Triads: see Figures 4.55–4.57.

FIGURE 4.55 Orange and Green

FIGURE 4.56   Green and Purple

FIGURE 4.57   Purple and Orange

- Tertiary Partial Triads: see Figures 4.58–4.60.

FIGURE 4.58   Red-Orange and Yellow-Green

FIGURE 4.59   Yellow-Green and Blue-Violet

FIGURE 4.60   Blue-Violet and Red-Orange

Bi-Chromatics with Neutrals

Two hues are distributed within a Neutral color scheme made up of variations of Greys, Blacks, Browns, Beiges, and/or Whites. The two hues may either be low-Contrast or high-Contrast in relation to one another. If choosing a high-Contrast combination, the result will be graphic and sharp, but also may be difficult to photograph accurately and/or fatigue the viewers' eyes. If choosing a low-Contrast combination, the result will appear more related, but also may be harder to see on stage under lights. More discussion of Color Contrast is contained in Chapter 7.

- Two hues plus White and Black: see Figures 4.61 and 4.62.

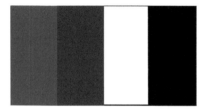

FIGURE 4.61 Blue, Purple, White, and Black

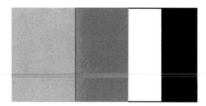

FIGURE 4.62 Turquoise, Pink, White, and Black

- Two hues plus Beige and Brown: see Figures 4.63 and 4.64.

FIGURE 4.63 Blue, Purple, Cream, and Brown

FIGURE 4.64   Turquoise, Pink, Cream, and Brown

Tri-Chromatic Harmonies

Tri-chromatic color schemes use three colors as the main hues. This may create either opposition or unity, depending on the relative size and purity of the three hues within the composition, and where the hues lie on the color wheel in relation to one another. These approaches may be further distinguished as follows:

Triad Color Harmonies

Triad colors are located at three equidistant points from one another around the color wheel. These may be the three Primary colors (Red, Blue, Yellow), Secondary colors (Orange, Green, Purple), or Tertiary colors (Red-Violet, Blue-Green, Yellow-Orange or Red-Orange, Yellow-Green, Blue-Violet). A triad color scheme will work for three characters of equivalent strength or a three-sided conflict, as using one color for each of three groups can create clear visual separation. Triad combinations based on Primary colors may be seen in children's toys or for comic effect.

Three hues of similar visual weight can also be distributed equally among a **group** of costumes. However, the colors generally will **not** be used equally within individual costumes except when a comic effect is the goal. Variations on these color harmonies include:

- Primary Triad: see Figure 4.65.

FIGURE 4.65   Red, Yellow, and Blue

- Adjusted Primary Triad: as with True Complements, Primary triad combinations are best used in limited spaces within a single costume in order to avoid a jarring effect. However, if the hues have their Values adjusted and/or are Neutralized, Subdued, or used in different proportions, the overall effect can be harmonious. These combinations work well when at least two of the three colors are altered from a full-intensity hue towards a more subdued result; see Figure 4.66.

FIGURE 4.66   Adjusted Primary Triad: Neutralized (Green added) Red, Yellow (White added) Tint, and Blue (Black added) Shade

- Secondary Triad: see Figure 4.67.

FIGURE 4.67   Orange, Green, and Purple

- Adjusted Secondary Triad: see Figure 4.68.

FIGURE 4.68   Orange (White added) Tint, Green (Black added) Shade, and Purple (Red added)

- Tertiary Triads: see Figures 4.69 and 4.70.
- Triad harmonies in unequal proportions: a Dominant/Supporting/Accent color scheme using unequal amounts of Triadic colors in altered form is often very useful. More exploration of this subject is contained in Chapter 5. See Figures 4.71–4.73.

FIGURE 4.69   Yellow–Green, Red–Orange, and Blue–Violet

FIGURE 4.70   Red–Violet, Blue–Green, and Yellow–Orange

FIGURE 4.71   Burgundy (Black added to Red), Navy (Black added to Blue), accent of Yellow

FIGURE 4.72   Eggplant (Black added to Purple), Sea Green (White and a small amount of Blue added to Green), accent of Peach (White added to Orange)

FIGURE 4.73   Olive Green (Red added to Green), Rust (Black added to Orange), accent of Lavender (White added to Purple)

Analogous Colors

Analogous colors are any three hues located next to one another on a color wheel. They have related undertones and coordinate well.

Analogous color harmonies have less contrast than Complementary and Triad schemes owing to the analogous colors' adjacent position on the color wheel, but they have more contrast than the Monochromatic schemes because they are made up of more than one hue. Analogous colors work well together in a fabric print because the hues have enough contrast to command attention, but are still related to one another by the middle color in the grouping.

Each of the groups in Figures 4.74–4.97 contains a common hue that unites all of the colors. This type of color grouping is useful for a chorus or group that does not need to be individualized. These color schemes include:

- Pure Analogous colors: see Figures 4.74–4.85.

FIGURE 4.74   Red, Red-Orange, and Orange

FIGURE 4.75   Red-Orange, Orange, and Yellow-Orange

FIGURE 4.76   Orange, Yellow-Orange, and Yellow

FIGURE 4.77   Yellow–Orange, Yellow, and Yellow–Green

FIGURE 4.78   Yellow, Yellow–Green, and Green

FIGURE 4.79   Yellow Green, Green, and Blue Green

FIGURE 4.80   Green, Blue-Green, and Blue

FIGURE 4.81   Blue-Green, Blue, and Blue-Violet

FIGURE 4.82 Blue, Blue–Violet, and Purple

FIGURE 4.83 Blue–Violet, Purple, and Red–Violet

FIGURE 4.84 Purple, Red–Violet, and Red

FIGURE 4.85 Red–Violet, Red, and Orange–Red

- Altered Analogous colors: for the most harmonious effect, choose one of the three hues in an Analogous color scheme as the Dominant color and use the others as Supporting colors or Accents. Add White to create a tint, Black to create a shade, Grey to add a tone, the hue's Complement for a Neutralized color, and/or add a different color for a Subdued color in at least one of the hues in the groupings, to avoid too much contrast. See Figures 4.86–4.97.

FIGURE 4.86   Red (with Black added), Orange (with Black added), and Yellow–Orange (with Black added)

FIGURE 4.87   Red-Orange (with Black added and Red reduced), Orange (with White added), and Yellow–Orange (Grey added and Saturation reduced)

FIGURE 4.88   Orange (with Black added and Red reduced), Yellow–Orange (Red was reduced, which tipped the original hue towards Green), and Yellow (White added)

FIGURE 4.89   Yellow–Orange (Black added), Yellow (White and Grey added), and Yellow–Green (Grey added and Saturation reduced)

FIGURE 4.90 Yellow (White and Grey were added), Yellow-Green (Green reduced), and Green (Black and Red were added). A small slice of the original Green was retained as an accent

FIGURE 4.91 Yellow-Green (Black added), Green (Black added), and Blue-Green (Black added). A small slice of the original Yellow-Green had White added and was retained as an accent

FIGURE 4.92 Green (Black and Grey added), Blue-Green (no change), and Blue (Black and a small amount of Grey added). A small slice of the original Green was retained as an accent

FIGURE 4.93 Blue-Green (no change), Blue (Black added and Red reduced), and Blue-Violet (Grey added). A small slice of the original Blue was retained as an accent

FIGURE 4.94   Blue, (White, Green, Black, and Grey added), Blue-Violet (Grey added), and Purple (Red and Black added)

FIGURE 4.95   Blue-Violet (no change), Purple (Black added), and Red-Violet (Grey added)

FIGURE 4.96   Purple (Grey added), Red-Violet (Grey and a small amount of Blue added), and Red (White added)

FIGURE 4.97   Red-Violet (Grey and Blue added), Red (Red reduced), and Orange-Red (Red reduced)

Split Complementary

Split Complementary color schemes combine a hue with the **hues on either side** of the true Complementary hue on the color wheel, but **not** the true Complement itself. As the two hues on either side of the true Complement will be Analogous hues to one another, the three colors in this combination will be weighted towards those two hues, and the third hue will be a Supporting or Accent color. This type of color scheme can give a nice uneven balance to the composition.

In the examples in Figures 4.98–4.103, the hues are all at high Saturation and of the same size. In a real costuming situation, it can be more harmonious to select one of the hues as the Dominant hue and then lower the Value or Intensity, Neutralize, and/or Subdue one or both of the other hues.

FIGURE 4.98   Red vs. Blue-Green and Yellow-Green

FIGURE 4.99   Green vs. Red-Violet and Red-Orange

FIGURE 4.100   Yellow vs. Blue-Violet and Red-Violet

FIGURE 4.101   Purple vs. Yellow-Orange and Yellow-Green

FIGURE 4.102 Orange vs. Blue–Violet and Blue–Green

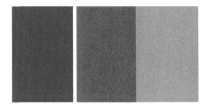

FIGURE 4.103 Blue vs. Red–Orange and Yellow–Orange

Four-Part or Tetrad Color Schemes

Four-part combinations can be hard to balance, although it is unlikely that any one character will wear all four colors at once and/or that the hues will be used in equal size or with an equal level of Saturation within a single costume.

Double Complementary

Double Complementary color harmonies utilize the two hues on **either side of both true complements**. For example, instead of Red vs. Green, Double Complements would be Red–Orange and Red–Violet vs. Yellow–Green and Blue–Green. The true Complements are **implied** but not shown.

- Double Complementary Schemes based on Primaries and Secondaries: see Figures 4.104–4.106.

FIGURE 4.104 Red and Purple vs. Green and Yellow

FIGURE 4.105   Yellow and Orange vs. Purple and Blue

FIGURE 4.106   Blue and Green vs. Orange and Red

• Double Complimentary Schemes based on Tertiaries: see Figures 4.107–4.109.

FIGURE 4.107   Red-Orange and Red-Violet vs. Blue-Green and Yellow-Green

FIGURE 4.108   Yellow-Green and Yellow-Orange vs. Blue-Violet and Red-Violet

FIGURE 4.109   Blue-Violet and Blue-Green vs. Red-Orange and Yellow-Orange

Notice that, within a Split Complementary combination, the pair of split complementary colors that are **close to one another on the color wheel** *and* **are tertiary color**s, such as Blue-Violet and Red-Violet, or Yellow-Green and Yellow-Orange, work well visually with one another. This is because there is a strong common undertone that relates the colors so that they don't "fight" **and** because Tertiary colors are mixed from a number of starting hues so that they are naturally somewhat subdued compared with full-intensity Primary colors. Once can make an attractive color scheme by using one of the two colors in such a pair as the Dominant color. Add a generous portion of light and dark Neutrals such as White and Black or Cream and dark Brown to surround these colors, and the colors will tend to work happily together.

At full Saturation/Intensity, many of the combinations above may seem very bright. Take note, in Figures 4.110 and 4.111, of how much calmer the colors look together when some or all of the hues have had their Values lowered or have been Neutralized or Subdued. The colors are also in different size relationships to one another, which helps the viewer make sense of what they are seeing because there is a hierarchy among the colors, which brings order. When all the hues are of equal Saturation and size, each color "fights" the others for dominance, and the viewer can be overwhelmed. Not all the possible combinations are pictured.

In a situation where full-Intensity colors will be used throughout the production, one can mitigate the chaotic effect by separating the bright colors with Neutrals such as White and Black, and by distributing accents of each of the hues around the composition.

FIGURE 4.110   Altered from 4.104. Red (Black added), Purple (Black added), Green (Black added), and Yellow (White added, then Grey)

FIGURE 4.111   Altered from 4.109. Red-Orange (Black added, saturation reduced), Red-Violet (Grey added), Blue-Green (Black added, Green reduced), and Yellow-Green (no change). Color positions were also changed on the page

FIGURE 4.112 Yellow-Green, Green, Blue-Green

FIGURE 4.113 White added as accents

FIGURE 4.114 Black added as accents

FIGURE 4.115 Colors distributed around the composition to break up large areas of saturated hues

Any of the approaches in this chapter can be used for a single costume or for an entire production. The single-costume approach will give a more unstudied effect and can be easier to achieve because the designer can focus on an important costume while using more subtle colors in the surrounding costumes. Conversely, using a distinct color scheme for **all** the costumes in a production will create a clear visual style that can be striking. However, an obvious color scheme can overwhelm a naturalistic production, appearing like the children in *The Sound of Music* in their costumes made of matching curtain fabrics. Keep the style of your production in mind as you select the color approach. The further away the production is from realism, the more stylized and obvious the use of colors can be.

5

OTHER METHODS OF CREATING A COLOR SCHEME

The model of a Color Wheel can be helpful for visualizing color relationships. However, once a designer is comfortable with the mechanics of color harmonies, they can begin to combine and balance colors to create a successful color scheme without specifically referring to the color wheel. Colors exist in relation to one another. Unless you choose to use a completely monochromatic color scheme in a single hue, you will be mixing colors. Therefore, it is helpful to look at how to combine colors harmoniously.

Playing with colors and seeing what "works" is the best teacher. The way to master color is through **practice**, whether by creating areas of color with pencils or markers on paper, mixing colors with watercolors or acrylic paint, combining colored fabric swatches, or using paint chips. Move the color samples around and try different combinations, different Intensities, and different Temperatures of hues. Vary the Proportions of colors in relation to one another. This chapter presents a variety of methods to make sense of color options.

Related Colors

Related colors have a **common undertone** that unites all of the hues and moves them towards one another. These colors appear to have been mixed with a single base color. For example, colors that are united by a Black, Beige, or Grey undertone will naturally seem to coordinate. Or, as discussed in Chapter 4, Analogous colors that are close together on the color wheel will share most of the same undertones, such as a Red-Orange and a Yellow-Orange, which are related by the Orange in both hues.

Closely related hues, at a distance, may appear as a larger block of a single hue and can tip the balance of the composition. Using this to your advantage, a large group of closely related hues can appear unified and less busy than a similarly sized arrangement of more contrasting hues. For a chorus, use related colors to create a sense of unity. At the same time, use a variety of fabric textures and garment shapes and different accent colors to avoid creating a group of characters who are wearing **related** colors but appear to be in **identical** hues.

Related Colors with a Common Undertone

FIGURE 5.1   Black, Blue-Grey, Blackened Red – related by Black

FIGURE 5.2   Tan, Beige, Peachy-Beige – related by Beige

FIGURE 5.3   Dark Taupe, Blue-Grey, Grey– related by Grey

FIGURE 5.4   Grey, dull Green, Grey-Brown – related by Grey

FIGURE 5.5   Grey, Mauve, pale cool Blue – related by pale Grey

FIGURE 5.6   Grey-Brown, Taupe, Slate – related by Grey

FIGURE 5.7   Blue-Grey, Charcoal, Black – related by Cool Grey

FIGURE 5.8   Slate Gray, Charcoal, Black – related by Grey

Related Colors with an Accent

Related colors can give an elegant effect. However, be careful that the hues are not **too** Subdued to hold their own under stage lights or against scenery colors. In that case, adding a somewhat contrasting **Accent Color** to the scheme can help add interest.

FIGURE 5.9   Black, Blue-Grey, Blackened Red with accents

FIGURE 5.10   Tan, Beige, Peachy-Beige with accents

FIGURE 5.11   Dark Taupe, Blue-Grey, Grey with accents

FIGURE 5.12   Grey, dull Green, Grey-Brown with accents

FIGURE 5.13   Grey, Mauve, pale cool Blue with accents

FIGURE 5.14   Grey-Brown, Taupe, Slate with accents

FIGURE 5.15   Blue-Grey, Charcoal, Black with accents

FIGURE 5.16 Slate Gray, Charcoal, Black with accents

Color Categories

Color Categories are a way of referring to groups of colors that have a similar aspect, such as color Saturation or Intensity (purity or brightness), color Value (on a scale from tints to shades), amount of contrast between colors, or the "mood" of the colors. Because every designer may group colors slightly differently, be sure to share your desired color swatches with the director and other designers so they understand your own definition of each of the terms. The groupings below are simplified; other color reference books may further subdivide each category or group the hues differently. For a discussion of how to combine different categories of color into a color scheme, please refer to Chapter 7.

- *Saturated, or Pure, Bold, and Bright Colors:* Pure and highly Saturated versions of the hues on a color wheel, or very Saturated versions of their tints.

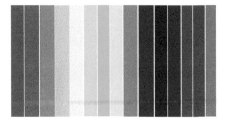

FIGURE 5.17 Color Wheel hues plus bright Pink, Magenta, and bright Teal.

- *Dark, Deep, or Rich Colors:* Deep colors are Shades in which hues have had Black mixed in with them. See figure 5.18.

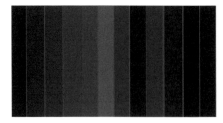

FIGURE 5.18 Blackened hues from the color wheel. Examples of Deep colors include Burgundy, Rust, Golden Ochre, deep Olive Green, Forest Green, Navy, Slate Blue, darkened Blue-Violet, and Eggplant.

- *Neon Colors*: Neon colors are extremely bright, with a "glow" that seems to emanate from within. They are best viewed on a computer monitor or with an internal light source. See figure 5.19.

FIGURE 5.19   Safety Orange, Neon Yellow, Lime Green, Electric Blue, and Hot Pink are examples of Neon colors. Note the Bold contrasts between these colors.

- *Soft, Light, or Pastel Colors*: Soft colors are also known as Tints, in which White is mixed with a hue. See figure 5.20.

FIGURE 5.20   Pale Rose, soft Coral, pale Peach, soft Yellow, soft Jade Green, Mint Green, pale Blue, pale Lilac, Lavender, and Pink.

- *Subdued or Greyed Colors*: Subdued or Greyed Tones of colors have had Grey (White and then a smaller amount of Black) and/or a little of the complementary hue mixed in to neutralize the color. See figure 5.21.
- *Medium Colors*: Slightly softened colors, Medium colors are not as bright as Saturated or Bold colors or as reduced as Pastels or Subdued colors. They make a good backbone to a color scheme. These colors appear somewhat faded compared with fully Saturated hues, but allow for variations within a color scheme because their Saturation may be increased or decreased from this starting point as needed. See figure 5.22.
- *Jewel Tones*: These are rich versions of hues that suggest the intense deep colors of precious stones. Jewel tones are often combined with metallic Gold or Silver. See figure 5.23.
- *Advancing Colors*: Advancing colors will take focus onstage and are best used for important characters or events in the script. Full-Saturation, Bright, High-value, Warm, and Neon colors tend to visually advance. In addition to their own saturated nature, using highly contrasting combinations of colors will

FIGURE 5.21 Saturated hues mixed with White, then Grey, and then altered further individually. Saturation was decreased, and Black was added in at the end for all colors shown. These colors include: Greyed Taupe (Greyed Red tint, Green added), Warm Taupe (Greyed Orange tint, saturation reduced, Grey added), Grey-Green (Greyed Green tint, Black added, saturation reduced), Dull Lavender (Greyed Blue tint, saturation reduced), Greyed Lilac (Greyed Purple tint, Grey added), Mauve (Greyed Pink tint, contrast reduced), and dull Brown (Greyed Pink tint, contrast reduced, Blue reduced on the computer to reveal more Orange, Black added).

FIGURE 5.22 Saturated hues from Figure 5.17, with 20% saturation reduced and 20% White added as the starting point for all colors. Soft Red, Rose (Red with additional White, Blue, and Black added), Orange, Yellow, Green, Turquoise, Medium Blue, Denim Blue (Black added to medium Blue, contrast reduced), faded Purple, dull Burgundy, softened Red-Violet, and Pink.

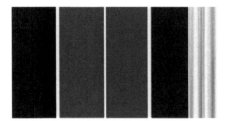

FIGURE 5.23 Ruby Red (increased Red, added Blue, added Black,), Emerald Green (full-intensity Green, added Black, increased saturation), Sapphire Blue (added Blue and Black, increased saturation, reduced Red), and Amethyst Purple (added Blue and Black, increased saturation). All colors had Black added again at the end. Metallic Silver and Gold are added as accents.

add to their advancing effect. Use advancing colors for characters that need to be seen more clearly, such as the main characters and characters around which other characters revolve. See figure 5.24.

FIGURE 5.24 Advancing colors

• *Receding Colors*: Cool colors tend to recede, as do low-Value, Darker, Neutralized (mixed with their Complement), or Subdued (mixed with another color to adjust) colors. Use receding colors for background characters, choruses, or to soften the effects of a Saturated color used elsewhere in the composition. These colors also tend to blend into one another because of their lack of contrast. See figure 5.25.

FIGURE 5.25 Receding colors

• *Warm Colors*: Warm colors are based on Red or Yellow and suggest fire or sunshine. These colors include Red, Orange, Yellow, Red-Orange, Yellow-Orange, and Yellow-Green. More discussion of color temperature is featured in Chapter 6. See figure 5.26.

FIGURE 5.26 Warm colors

- *Cool Colors*: Cool colors are based on Blue and suggest water. These colors include Green, Blue-Green, Blue, Blue-Violet, Purple, and greyed Red-Violet. See figure 5.27.

FIGURE 5.27 Cool colors

- *Natural Colors*: Natural hues are taken from the colors of stones, tree bark, sand, leaves, and grass. These colors tend to be toned down from pure hues and mix well together. Of course, where one lives in the world will affect one's perception of what colors are "natural." Different plant varieties, different colors of soil, and different types of foliage will appear different to the viewer, as warmer climates tend to have a Yellow tone in the light and in the leaves. For locations at higher latitudes, the light may be Greyer, the leaves more of a Blue-Green, and even the rocks and sand may appear Blue-Grey. See figure 5.28.

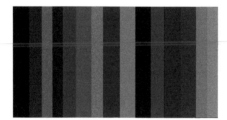

FIGURE 5.28 Natural colors

- *Autumn Colors*: Warm, dark hues are considered Autumnal, such as Pumpkin Orange, Rust Red, warm Brown, Ochre Gold, along with accents of deep Forest Green or Olive Green of surrounding vegetation and the Blue of the autumn sky. See figure 5.29.
- *Spring Colors*: Spring colors include clear medium hues and pastels, such as might be seen in flowers, leaves, and the Spring sky. See figure 5.30.
- *Patriotic Colors*: Colors taken from the national flag or symbols of a particular country. Remember, an audience will tend to associate a certain set of colors with their own nation, even if the colors also pertain to another nation. For

FIGURE 5.29   Autumn colors

FIGURE 5.30   Spring colors

example, Red, White, and Blue will automatically suggest France, the United Kingdom, or the United States to different audiences.

- *Neutral Colors*: Neutral colors blend easily with and support more-Saturated colors, without having a defined color personality of their own.
  - Light Neutrals Figure 5.31

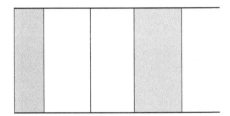

FIGURE 5.31   Light Neutrals: Pale Grey, White, Beige, pale Warm Grey, Cream

  - Medium Neutrals Figure 5.32

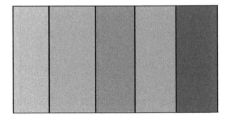

FIGURE 5.32   Medium Neutrals: Warm Grey, medium Grey, Cool Grey, Greened Taupe, medium Grey-Brown

- Dark Neutrals Figure 5.33

FIGURE 5.33 Dark Neutrals: Grey, Brown, Grey-Brown, Charcoal, dark Cool Grey, dark Warm Grey, Black, Dull Black

- *Neutralized and Subdued Colors*: These colors have been toned down and reduced from their full intensities, generally by addition of their complements to the original hue (Neutralized colors) or by addition of another color for the purpose of reducing the intensity of the original hue (Subdued colors). These colors can work for suiting, shoes, and furniture, where a too-bright color would draw too much focus. See figure 5.34.

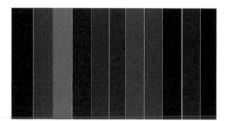

FIGURE 5.34 Deep Neutralized and Subdued colors: Cordovan, Rust, Luggage Tan, Forest Green, Olive drab, dark Taupe, Slate Blue-Grey, Sage Green, Navy, Sepia, and Chocolate

"Lines" of Color

A similar color or category of colors is often chosen for an individual character throughout their costume changes. With a clear through-line of color, it is easier to maintain a color scheme over the course of a production. As most people in real life tend to favor certain colors and to choose variations on those colors throughout their wardrobes, a character may be designed in a tight range of colors throughout the play.

The through-line color may get stronger or weaker as a character's fortunes wax or wane. If there are strong reversals or changes to a character in the play, the character may be put in a much more- or less-Saturated version of the through-line color or in a completely different color to illustrate this change. For example, a designer may contrast two characters by using Rusts and Reds in their costumes. As one prospers, their Rusts get more vibrant and their Reds get clearer; as the other character diminishes, their colors become more Greyed and sad.

Related or Analogous colors can then be used to indicate relationships between the main character and other characters, such as lovers, family members, friends, and follower groups, based on the similarities or changing relationships of colors between the main character and others around them. See Chapter 11 for a fuller discussion of using colors to signal character relationships, and Chapter 13 for a discussion of costume changes within a color scheme.

Another way of using this method is to purposely contrast each character by choosing a clear line of color for them that is not seen on other characters. In Heather Raffo's *Nine Parts of Desire*, a group of Iraqi women discuss their lives under the rule of President Saddam Hussein and during the two wars with the United States. The women are united by wearing a black abaya, a long, enveloping garment that makes them undistinguishable on the street, but are clearly different when they are at home and remove the abaya, showing the range of their personalities and experiences.

FIGURE 5.35 *Nine Parts of Desire* costumes. The upper register shows the characters in the abaya worn on the streets. The lower register shows the characters as individuals, using different colors to represent their range of personalities: an American woman of Iraqi descent; Umm Ghada, who mourns a daughter killed by an American bombing; an Iraqi girl who loves American boy bands and doesn't understand politics; Amal, a Bedouin woman who is disappointed in love; Huda, an exiled intellectual in London who protested the Hussein regime; Layal, an artist who depends on the regime for support of her work; and Nanna, an older woman who survives by selling stolen Iraqi artifacts

Color Repeats

An Accent color may be chosen to unite a scene, no matter how varied the costumes' colors are as a whole. This is an especially good method for unifying a large group of pulled or rented costumes. For example, an array of costumes in a variety of medium tones can be pulled together through repeated accents of a strong color such as Red used in accessories, jewelry, hat trims, fabric prints, garment edging, shawls, scarves, sashes, and belts. The repeated accents of a single hue will lead the viewers' eyes around the group of characters and create a sense of unity.

Focused Contrast

By using a contrasting fully Saturated hue in a color scheme, a designer may indicate an important moment or a meaningful costume. To be most effective, it is best to refrain from using the chosen color elsewhere in the costumes or scenery. For example, this technique is often used when there will be stage blood used at a crucial moment, as blood will be more striking when it appears in a production where clear Red has been "saved" and has not been used in the color palette before the blood is seen.

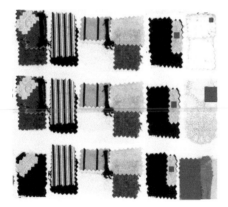

FIGURE 5.36 Colors for a production of *Dracula*. The overall palette of Black, White, and Grey is contrasted with a small area of Red on Dracula's costume and Red accents that get larger for Lucy's garments as she falls increasingly under Dracula's power from Acts 1 to 3. Left to right, the colors represent the three acts of the play for Dr. Seward, the maid, the manservant, Dr. Van Helsing, Dracula, and Lucy

Images from the Script

Strong images from the script may suggest a color approach. In this case, if an image is repeated or is important in the written script, it may be the starting point for a color scheme. As discussed in Chapter 1, the title character in *Hamlet* is spoken of as wearing Black, while others are in bolder tones to celebrate the recent wedding of Claudius and Gertrude.

However, there are times when the direction or production style doesn't lend itself to using the hue(s) mentioned in the script. In this situation, the Costume Designer should alert the director so that the decision can be made to either cut, alter, or ignore the spoken line(s).

Metaphors

Images or metaphors that illustrate the characters or action, but are not specifically mentioned in the script, can suggest colors. Metaphors are useful when the metaphor helps limit the color scheme to the colors contained within the mental image. For example, the opera *Così Fan Tutte* features two young people who foolishly flirt with their disguised sweethearts and fall in love with the wrong person. For a production of the opera, the costume designer used **peacocks** as a metaphor for beautiful creatures who exist in a sheltered garden. A color scheme of Purple, Blue, Lavender, Teal, and Olive greens, with Rose Pink accents, was used for the young lovers' costumes.

FIGURE 5.37   *Così Fan Tutte* costumes for Guglielmo, Fiordiligi, Ferrando, and Dorabella

As a metaphor is imposed **on** the script rather than arising as an image from **within** the script, it is important that all the designers and director agree on the same metaphor so that there is visual cohesion. In the *Così* example, the set designer proposed a lush, walled garden, the director embraced the idea, and the costume designer suggested using peacocks as a starting point for the characters. Metaphors allow a design team to find a visual language to communicate moods and ideas to the audience.

Visual Image

Color can be taken from a visual image that **suggests** the theme or mood of the play. Photographs or paintings of landscapes or architecture may be the starting point for a successful color scheme because the hues in the image tend to be related in some manner (figure 5.38). Decorative arts such as ceramics or small textiles may also be great inspirations, although it is good to be careful with these sources – they are often intended to be small accents in a large space and may be too intense for a whole group of costumes or scenery! Best to use these sources for a special costume or for decorative scenic touches.

When starting with a visual image, pay attention to the **proportions** of hues in the artwork as well as the specific hues. Note the proportions of colors and of neutrals, how the hues relate to one another, the use of stronger colors as accents, and how the colors lead your eye to a focal point. If the entire design team is using the same visual image, be sure to discuss each designer's take on the sources so that the design team will end up working on the same color story, but in such a way that the costumes, scenery, and lighting are not so close that they all blend together on stage. For more discussion of using a color source as inspiration, refer to Chapter 9.

FIGURE 5.38   London spiral photograph used as a reference image to create a color scheme

Orchestration

One can approach colors as if they were aspects of music. This is especially useful for a designer with Synesthesia, although they may "hear" color differently from what is described here. By orchestrating color, one will use the **individual hues as an overall composition**, with Medium tones as the main melody, Dark shades as the base/low notes, Light tints and/Advancing colors as the high notes, Saturated colors as accents, and Subdued colors as counterpoints.

A Dominant color or group of colors can act as a repeated motif, as in a musical composition, that harkens back to earlier moments in the play or creates a through-line for a character and/or group of characters by being repeated in different Values and levels of Saturation. For example, in Figure 5.39, the Purple color samples start as a near-Black and progress up to a dark Amethyst Jewel tone, Medium Purple, full-Saturation Purple, and Advancing Purple. A very high-Value tint of Purple or even White may be used as an accent if the designer needs a contrast with otherwise dark shades, or the Advancing Saturated Purple may be used if the designer needs a contrast with otherwise Neutralized or Subdued colors used elsewhere.

Any color scheme, group of existing garments, or fabrics may be coordinated with this method. This orchestration approach works very well with a show for which you are pulling and shopping many of the costume items, as it helps you choose accents, accessories, shirts, shoes, and other garments to fill out the color range to get a fuller visual symphony. Looking at Figure 5.39, the lower registers, or "low notes," start with the darkest-Value and lowest-Saturation colors and gradually increase in Saturation and Value towards small amounts of accent colors, which may be Advancing saturated hues or light Neutrals, depending on the other colors used in the composition.

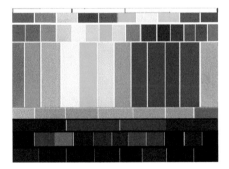

FIGURE 5.39   Orchestrated color array. The arrangement of color categories, representing low notes up to high notes, is bottom to top: Dark Neutrals, Dark Subdued and Neutralized colors, Jewel tones, Subdued colors, Medium colors as the most used "melody," Saturated hues, Advancing colors, and Light Neutrals

Inherent Rhythm

The inherent rhythm in the play can be translated into the visual rhythm of color usage. Greek tragedies tend to be stately and formal. This may be expressed with a color scheme made up of unified, neutralized colors for the chorus and solid deep colors for the main characters. Conversely, farces tend to be quick and energetic. A farce's high-energy bounciness may be suggested by the way color makes the viewers' eyes move around the stage, such as using large areas of bright colors of similar intensity. The rhythm of the production can be visually represented through:

• Using Neutralized, Subdued, Deep, and Dark Neutral colors for a stately effect, or Advancing and Saturated colors for a bouncy effect, using the Color Categories described earlier in this chapter. See figures 5.40–5.41.

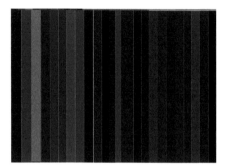

FIGURE 5.40   Stately effect, using Neutralized colors, Deep colors, and dark Neutrals. Not all colors in the original categories are included here, and some of the higher-Value colors in this array were darkened to reduce contrast for less of a "break" between colors, which helps create a steady **flow**

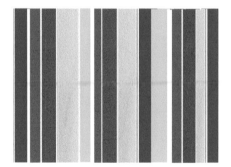

FIGURE 5.41   Bouncy effect, using Advancing and Saturated colors. The colors were rearranged to increase contrast between them and to create repeats, although each sequence is slightly different. The addition of white borders, combined with different widths of colors, leads the viewer's eye to **hop** from one color repeat to the next

• Combining Bold or Subtle color **contrasts within a single costume**. The Bold contrasts will bounce the eye back and forth between blocks of colors and may visually "cut" the wearer's figures into blocks. The Subtle contrasts lead the eye around the figure in a fluid, continuous line, creating a calm impression and a more unified figure. See figures 5.42–5.43.

FIGURE 5.42   Bold contrasts within a costume. A variety of Saturated colors lead the eye to search for color repeats around the composition, creating a scattered effect. In addition, strong contrast creates a visual "break" where two colors meet

FIGURE 5.43   Subtle contrasts within a costume. The colors are closely related in Saturation and Value, creating more unity in the composition. Off-White accents are added for interest in order to keep the composition from blending together **too** much

- Using the **size** of each color area to draw focus, whether by using equal-sized large areas of bright contrasting colors of similar intensity so that the colors visually "fight" one another, or by designing a large dominant color area with subtle supporting colors that will create unity with some variety. See Figures 5.44–5.45.
- Adding bands of edging, graphic patterns, or color breakups to create **small areas of interest** that repeat within a costume to suggest the script rhythm. See Figure 5.46.
- Repeating hues throughout a group of costumes but using the colors in **different locations** on different costumes, so that the viewer's eye moves from one area of the hue to the next around the entire stage picture in a particular rhythm. See figure 5.47.

FIGURE 5.44 Saturated contrasting colors in equal-sized blocks. The eye tends to toggle between the two hues where they meet

FIGURE 5.45 Related colors of different sizes. The large Blue area is clearly the dominant area, with subdued Orange and a Blue shade colors as supporting accents. Repeating the accent at the upper edge helps the eye move up and down the figure. Adding vertical blue stripes would enhance this effect even more

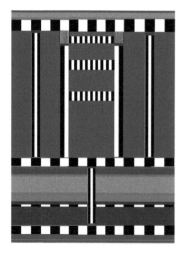

FIGURE 5.46 Repeated variations of Black and White checks, used as trim to lead the eye around the composition

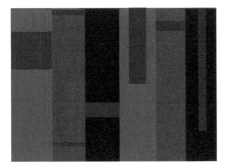

FIGURE 5.47   Repeated hues in different locations on a group of costumes

Dominant, Supporting, and Accent Colors

For overall unity no matter which colors you choose, the color **distribution** and **proportions** should be carefully thought out. When it comes time to make specific color choices, the framework discussed below can help a designer make choices about how to distribute colors, whether in a group of costumes or in one specific costume.

A very useful approach for a color scheme is to choose three colors that reflect the intended mood, style, and approach to the play. These three colors – hereafter called the Base colors – should look good together. Build the color scheme around them with variations of Saturation, Value, Placement, and Size.

- Take one color and build the color composition around it. This is the Dominant or Main color. Consider the Intensity and the Value of the Dominant color and repeat it throughout the costumes. The Dominant color may be Deep, Saturated, Subdued, or High-Value, depending on the production. For a stylized production, the Dominant color will be repeated in the **same** Intensity and Value throughout the costumes. For a more naturalistic production, **vary** the Intensity, Value, and Size of the Dominant color, or use colors that **are similar but not identical to** the Dominant color, such as Related colors, to repeat throughout the costumes in order to create a less-composed look. **The Dominant color will make up approximately 55–60% of the composition**.
- Add a Supporting color that contrasts with, enhances, or coordinates with the Dominant color. The Supporting color may either be Bolder or more Neutralized than the Dominant color. **The Supporting color will make up approximately 30–35% of the composition**.
- Finally, add an Accent or a "Pop" color, which will be bolder and have more Contrast with the other two colors, but will be used in a focused area. Think of this color as a dash of spice added to the composition, enlivening it and giving it interest. Use the Accent color in small areas for accessories such

as jewelry, prints on fabric, belts, hats, gloves, shoes, hair accessories, neckties, scarves, or other finishing touches. **The Accent color will make up approximately 10% of the composition**.

When combining colors within a single costume, a subtle color scheme can be created if the Dominant color is more Neutralized in the largest area, with a more Saturated supporting color in a smaller area, and with an Accent Saturated color in a small area near the face.

For example, use a large area of Neutralized color for a suit, dress, or jacket. Add a second color for a smaller area such as a shirt, blouse, vest, or bodice inset. This second color should be bolder than the suiting color. You may use a Supporting color that is flattering to the wearer near the wearer's face, to counteract a suit or costume color that does not flatter the actor's coloring.

Finally, use repeated small areas of a third color as an Accent color to create interest with accessories such as jewelry, belts, hats, gloves, scarves, neckties, prints on fabric, trims, or as other finishing touches. The Accent color can be used to "bridge" two other colors in a combination. An example of this is using an Accent garment such as a scarf to separate and buffer two colors that don't look harmonious when placed right next to one another but that coordinate well enough to mix in a costume.

To use this same idea across an entire group of costumes, choose one or more of the three Base colors, in a very Neutralized form, for the suiting components or other large costume areas that do not need to draw attention. Use more Saturated versions of the three Base hues from your scheme as Supporting colors to add interest to the suiting components with shirts, blouses, vests, or other subordinate smaller garments. Finally, use a bolder version of the Base hues in small areas as Accent or "Pop" colors for accessories such as jewelry, prints on fabric, belts, hats, gloves, neckties, scarves, or other finishing touches.

Possible suit ensembles based on Blue and Grey or Tan and Brown color combinations with Red spectrum accents include:

- Grey gabardine suit, White cotton or silk top, Black patterned embroidered scarf or black patterned necktie with Magenta accents.
- Blue suit, pale Grey cashmere sweater, Navy silk scarf or necktie with White pin dots, Red accessories.
- Tan suit, Cream piqué top, Brown and Cream tweed scarf or necktie, Rust accessories.

For a more naturalistic result within a noticeable color scheme, the Accent colors may be different for different characters.

When using the three Base colors in an overall costume design, use contrasts in the Values, Saturation, Size, and Placement of the colors as you repeat them in the composition.

Prints and patterns can be used to extend the color scheme and to add visual interest. Prints should incorporate at least **two** of the chosen hues, or a Saturated version of one of the chosen hues plus a Neutral such as White, Cream, Beige, Tan, dark Brown, Navy, Grey, or Black.

Using Neutralized Hues in a Dominant/ Supporting/Accent Scheme

To create a sense of unity between costumes, concentrate on two to three hues and repeat those in variations of Intensity, Pattern, and Position on the body.

Make sure that the main characters stand out in this grouping, either with slightly Brighter or more Saturated colors, or with colors that are slightly different than any other characters' colors. Characters who need to work together onstage may be put in colors that coordinate, or in the very same colors if the colors are repeated in different places on the costume. Finish the costumes with smaller areas of a strong Accent color to add drama.

The Dominant/Supporting/Accent approach can create a harmonious blend of two very contrasting colors, including Complements, if you Shade or Neutralize one of the colors, and/or use the colors in different sizes. Choose one color in the group as the Dominant color and use the other in a smaller area in a smaller proportion as a Supporting color, in either a purer or neutralized version of the color. Add Accent colors to the color scheme to add interest.

When creating a color scheme, the different combinations of Saturated and Neutralized colors may extend a color scheme in different costumes by using the same Hues. For example, in the Red and Green grouping, one character may be in Burgundy and Green, another in Burgundy and Forest, another in Green and Burgundy, and a fourth in Forest and Burgundy. Not all the possible groupings are shown below; refer to Chapter 4 for more combinations of Neutralized and full-Saturation colors to which accent colors may be added.

* Red and Green

FIGURE 5.48 60% Burgundy (shade of Red), 30% Green, 10% Accents

FIGURE 5.49 60% Forest Green (shade of Green), 30% Red, 10% Accents

FIGURE 5.50 60% Burgundy (shade of Red), 30% Forest Green (shade of Green), 10% Accents

FIGURE 5.51 60% Forest Green (shade of Green), 30% Burgundy (shade of Red), 10% Accents

- Orange and Blue

FIGURE 5.52 60% Rust (shade of Orange), 30% Blue, 10% Accents

FIGURE 5.53 60% Navy (shade of Blue), 30% Orange, 10% Accents

FIGURE 5.54 60% Rust (shade of Orange), 30% Navy (shade of Blue), 10% Accents

FIGURE 5.55 60% Navy (shade of Blue), 30%, Rust (shade of Orange), 10% Accents

- Yellow and Purple

FIGURE 5.56 60% Yellow, 30% Eggplant (shade of Purple), 10% Accents

FIGURE 5.57 60% Eggplant (shade of Purple), 30% Yellow, 10% Accents

FIGURE 5.58 60% Golden Ochre (shade of Yellow), 30% Eggplant (shade of Purple), 10% Accents

FIGURE 5.59 60% Eggplant (shade of Purple), 30% Golden Ochre (shade of Yellow), 10% Accents

Although the Color Wheel is a great starting point for understanding color relationships, the best way to learn about color is to experiment to find color combinations that you like **before** you need them.

Take notice of how colors play off one another in store displays, in nature, in food markets, in cars, in house exteriors, and in advertising. When you start to closely look at how colors are combined in various ways around you each day, you will become more sensitive to how colors can combine to create different moods and impressions. The relative Size, Placement, and Intensity of colors will affect how the overall composition registers with the viewer, leads their eye towards a focal point, and evokes emotion.

Once you have some color inspirations, try combining colors: in outfits that you can wear, or in how you arrange food on a plate, or by moving color samples around to see which colors look good to you. Some people test out colors by painting with watercolors or acrylic; I love to play with arranging fabrics in a fabric store as I shop, or by playing with paint sample cards when I need to be inspired. Notice how changing the Placement of hues may alter how well the colors seem to coordinate, and how your eye is led around the combination. Also notice how changing one color in a group may entirely change the mood or apparent cohesiveness of the composition. Get comfortable playing with colors, with trying to reproduce the mood of a striking combination that inspires you, and with testing out how colors work together.

6

COLOR TEMPERATURE

Color can appear Warm or Cool. Warm colors are based on Red and/or Yellow and have a sense of sunshine and fire. Orange, a mix of Red and Yellow, is therefore also a Warm color. Cool colors are based on Blue. Blue, Green, and Purple have a sense of water, refreshment, and crispness. Green, which combines Blue with Yellow, and Purple, which combines Blue with Red, can be Warmer or Cooler based on the proportions of Blue to Yellow or Red in the mix.

Combinations of Colors, Based on Color Temperatures with a Neutral

Lovely color combinations can be created with a Warm color, a Cool color, and a Neutral. These combinations will look best if one color is used as the Dominant color and comprises more than half the proportion of the overall figure, with a Supporting color of a lesser size, and the third color as an Accent in a small area.

With each of the combinations shown in Figure 6.1–6.6, **the proportions can be changed for individual costumes, while the same over-all color scheme is maintained to create cohesion within a group**. This is also useful if a character needs to change costumes but maintain a similar look. In figures 6.6-6.7, instead of changing hues, the new costume may use **different proportions** of the character's consistent color scheme. More discussion of Costume Changes is contained in Chapter 13.

Varying Color Temperatures for Each Hue

Most hues have both **Warm** and **Cool** versions. For example, Red is thought of as inherently Warm, but specific Reds can be Cool, as in Maroon or Burgundy.

FIGURE 6.1   Peach, Mint Green, and Beige

FIGURE 6.2   Rust, Forest Green, and Taupe

FIGURE 6.3   Deep Rose, deep Leaf Green, and Cream

FIGURE 6.4   Burgundy, Forest Green, and Charcoal

FIGURE 6.5   Apple Green, Greyed Lavender, and soft Grey

FIGURE 6.6   Red, dark Navy, and White

Blue is considered to be inherently Cool, but can be warmed up to a Teal Blue-Green. All Warm colors can be cooled down, and all Cool colors can be warmed up, if the base hue has a cooler or warmer adjacent color mixed in.

Neutrals may appear either Warm or Cool, and, depending on the other hues in a specific color combination, the very same neutral colors can be considered **both** Cool and Warm in different instances, such as Taupe, Umber, Chocolate, or Charcoal. With all of these colors, the perceived color will be relative, depending on how warm or cool the colors adjacent to these hues are. Placing a very cool Pink next to a Pink that is less cool will make the second hue appear warmer.

FIGURE 6.7   Red bodice, White and Blue patterned skirt

FIGURE 6.8   Blue bodice, Red skirt

If the design team has been sharing a color inspiration source, and you find that the set and costume colors are too close, consider adjusting the intensity of the costume colors and/or switching to the other temperature of the color. For example, if there will be a large sky-Blue area on the set, consider Navy (shade of Blue) or Teal (Blue mixed with Green for a warmer effect) for the costumes.

Color Temperatures

Hue	Warm		Cool	

Red

FIGURE 6.9 Lacquer Red, Fire engine Red, Red-Orange

FIGURE 6.10 Ruby Red, Raspberry, Burgundy

Pink

FIGURE 6.11 Strawberry, Salmon, bright Pink

FIGURE 6.12 Cool Pink, pale Pink, deep Rose, Mauve Pink. Despite being a tint of Red, Pinks often appear Cool

Orange/ Rust

FIGURE 6.13 Orange, Rust, Apricot

FIGURE 6.14 Cool Orange, dull Rust, Rosy Peach

Yellow

FIGURE 6.15 Bright Yellow, Butter Yellow, Sunflower, bright Golden Ochre

FIGURE 6.16 Cool Yellow, pale Yellow, dull Golden Ochre. Cool yellows often appear somewhat Green

Hue	Warm		Cool	

Green				

FIGURE 6.17 Green, Yellow–Green, bright Green

FIGURE 6.18 Cool Green, Blue–Green, Forest

Blue				

FIGURE 6.19 Blue Green, Caribbean Blue, Turquoise

FIGURE 6.20 Blue, Greyed Blue, Navy

Purple/ Violet				

FIGURE 6.21 Red Violet, Plum, bright Fuchsia

FIGURE 6.22 Blue-Purple, Periwinkle, Lavender, deep Plum

Neutral Colors by Temperature

Hue	Warm		Cool	

White				

FIGURE 6.23 Off-White, Cream, Ecru Winter White

FIGURE 6.24 Snow White, Pure White, Blue-White

(*Continued*)

(*Continued*)

Hue	Warm		Cool	

Beige/Tan

FIGURE 6.25 Golden Tan, Warm Beige, Khaki, Caramel Tan

FIGURE 6.26 Greyed Beige, Taupe, deep Taupe

Brown

FIGURE 6.27 Warm Brown, Chocolate, Sienna

FIGURE 6.28 Dusty Brown, Coffee, Brown Grey

Grey

FIGURE 6.29 Warm Grey, Brown Grey

FIGURE 6.30 Charcoal, Blue Grey Black

FIGURE 6.31 Warm Black, Deep Umber

FIGURE 6.32 Cool Black, Blue Black

Color Temperatures and the Wearer

The skin, hair, and eye colors of the wearer should be factored into color choices, at least for those hues worn near the face. Clothing colors **reflect onto** skin tones, and clothing colors **contrast with** hair colors. Too bright a hue can overwhelm a pale actor; too warm a hue is hard for an actor with a ruddy pink complexion to wear attractively; too dull a hue can drain the complexion of someone with subtle coloring; too cool a color can make some people look ill; and too dark a hue can either overwhelm or blend into skin and hair tones. In these cases, adjusting the color Value or Temperature of a particular hue may make it more flattering to the wearer. However, on the stage, a designer may use colors on an actor that might be unflattering in real life by adjusting makeup and wig colors. For more discussion of using colors to flatter actors, see Chapter 12.

7

COLOR CONTRASTS

For all of the color combinations discussed in Chapters 4–6, Color Contrasts are inherent to their structure. Color Contrast refers to the **visual difference between two or more hues in a composition**. The further away the hues are from one another on the color wheel, the higher the Contrast. Complementary color schemes, using opposite colors on the color wheel such as Red and Green, Orange and Blue, or Purple and Yellow, have the most contrast because there are absolutely no common colors between the pairs of hues. Split complementary and double complementary schemes are high-contrast but have a small amount of commonality in at least two of the hues and are therefore less contrasting than true complements. Triads have somewhat less contrast, analogous and related colors are more similar because they have a common undertone, and monochromatic color harmonies are the most similar because they are based on a single hue.

Contrast is also affected by the relative Values and amount of Saturation within colors in a group. A high-Value color and a low-Value color used together will have more contrast than two high- or two low-Value colors, and a high-Saturation color with another high-Saturation color will have more contrast than a high-Saturation color with a Neutralized or Subdued lower-Saturation color or two low-Saturation colors used together.

Use the level of contrast within the color scheme to express the mood of a production, whether muted and monochromatic, soft, light and bright, medium, or bold and vibrant. In general, **the greater the contrast of Value and Saturation between colors, the Bolder the effect will be. The Softer the contrast, the Subtler the effect will be.**

When designing for the theatre, remember that color contrasts generally need to be **increased from the level that one would wear in daily life**. Colored stage lighting has a tendency to blend costume hues closer together. The larger the stage and theatre space, the more the costume colors will appear to be similar if they are not right next to one another. Subtle color contrasts can work in movie or television close-ups, but, in theatre, noticeable color contrasts are helpful in allowing the audience to discern different colors and details.

Also keep in mind the amount of contrast in the actors' own coloring. A person with a dark complexion and dark brown hair or a pale complexion and light ashen hair will have a low-contrast appearance; a person with an olive medium-tone complexion and black hair or with a very pale complexion and red or medium brown hair will have medium contrast; and a pale-complected person with dark brown hair or a dark-complected person with light blond hair will have high contrast. Try to use the costume and makeup colors to keep the amount of contrast onstage strong enough that the actors may be seen against the scenery, but not so much that it appears distracting. Work to have at least **one level of contrast difference** between the actor and the costume colors. In practice, this means using medium contrasts within a costume on a low-contrast or high-contrast person, and low- or high-contrasts within a costume on a medium-contrast person.

Contrast and Placement

Two or more different colors laid next to one another will have some level of contrast, which can be used to design advantage. In any color scheme, the level of contrast can be increased by adding both Warm and Cool colors; by using Primary colors rather than Tertiary colors because of the greater relative Intensity of a Primary color as compared with a Tertiary color; by using very different Values of colors; by using large areas of Saturated colors next to one another; or by using shiny or reflective textures. Contrast can be reduced by using the same color Temperature and similar color Values, choosing Neutralized hues, adding a Neutral buffer color between two hues, using the colors in small prints rather than in solids, or by using flat or matte surfaces.

Color contrasts are stronger at the point that two colors meet. The sharper the contrast between two colors that are positioned right next to one another, the more they will visually vibrate and be clearly different from one another. The principle of **Simultaneous Contrast** refers to the perception that the same color will appear Darker if it is adjacent to a Light color, Lighter if it is adjacent to a Dark color, and more Saturated if it is adjacent to its color Complement (for example, Redder if it is adjacent to Green, or Bluer if it is adjacent to Orange). Using Purple as a sample, you can see the results in Figures 7.1–7.3:

FIGURE 7.1   Purple and tint

FIGURE 7.2   Purple and shade

FIGURE 7.3   Purple and complement

Conversely, the further two colors are physically positioned away from one another, the more similar they will appear. In other words, colors that do **not** touch but are very similar will look **more** similar as the physical distance between them increases. For example, wearing a Blue shirt can bring out the color of Blue eyes, but Blue eye shadow worn right next to the eyes might show that the eyes themselves are not purely Blue. When one looks at many of the color samples in this book, similar colors that are not located right next to each other in a single grouping may look like a repeat of the same color, despite the fact that the hues are different.

The concept of "declining color differences over space" is useful for creating visual unity. By repeating similar strong hues, such as warm Reds, at least three times against a background of low-intensity colors such as Beiges or Grey, the different Reds will appear to be the same and appear to be used intentionally. In this case, the spectators' eyes will tend to jump from Red spot to Red spot, creating movement while seeking out the "like" colors. This method works both within a single costume and with a large group of characters on stage.

A color repeated at least three times in a costume or a group of costumes will create unity, even if the area of each repeat is small. This is a good rule for using Accent colors in small areas – repeat the small Accent several times to reduce the shock of a strong color contrast and to make it look as if the color has been planned. See figure 7.4. If the color repeats occur along a vertical axis within an individual costume, this will create a vertical line in the figure. See figure 7.5.

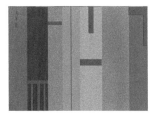

FIGURE 7.4 Scattered repeats of Red draw focus against low-value costumes and create unity

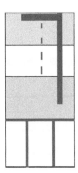

FIGURE 7.5 Vertical accents

Closely related hues worn near one another **will appear from a distance** to be a large block of a single hue, which can tip the balance of the composition. A chorus of characters in a range of Browns, Golds, and Tans will tend to visually blend together into a larger block of Neutrals that sets off smaller areas of brighter or lighter colors on the principal characters. See figure 7.6.

FIGURE 7.6 Tan background with brighter costume

Contrast with the Background

Backgrounds, whether made up of scenery or created by crowds of characters, will influence how costume colors are perceived. A Red costume is generally considered to be bright, but a Red costume in front of a Red-Brown brick wall is harder to see than a Blue costume would be, because Blue has a higher contrast with the Red-Brown wall than does Red. However, the Red of the costume will also appear less Brown than usual, as the Brown of the Red-Brown brick wall will make the Red of the dress even sharper. See figures 7.7–7.8.

FIGURE 7.7 Brick wall with red costume

FIGURE 7.8 Brick wall with blue costume

Saturation and Value

Color contrasts will be affected by a combination of Saturation and Value. As the two factors are adjusted against one another, a costume color can be made more or less visible on a given background.

The apparent Saturation, or Intensity, of a color will be affected by the background. A highly Saturated costume against a low-Contrast, low-Saturation background will be very noticeable. A highly Saturated costume on a high-Contrast, more Saturated background has to be chosen carefully to stand out and not to clash. In this case, it is best to use a costume color that will contrast with the prevailing colors of the set – the Intensity of the color sample that was used here to illustrate this point needed to be increased several times from what appeared to be a very bright color when used in Figure 7.10, in order to be clearly visible in Figure 7.12.

FIGURE 7.9 Red-Violet appears in high Contrast against a low-Intensity background

FIGURE 7.10 The same Red-Violet used in Figure 7.9 has less visual contrast with a higher-Intensity background

FIGURE 7.11   Red-Violet color from figure 7.9, with added Saturation on the computer to increase its visibility against a higher-Intensity background

FIGURE 7.12   Red-Violet color with added Saturation and Red increased 100% and Blue increased 50% on the computer to increase its visibility even more against the background

A high-Saturation color used against a high-Value, low Saturation background will be clearly visible, whereas the same color will be visible but somewhat absorbed into a low-Contrast, low-Value background.

FIGURE 7.13   Low-Contrast, high-Value background, with a full-Saturation Red-Violet

FIGURE 7.14   Low-Contrast, low-Value background, with the same Red-Violet variation from Figure 7.13

Low-Saturation Subdued colors used both in the background and on a garment will muddle together and be hard to see, and a low-Saturation garment against a highly Saturated background will look even Greyer than it already is.

A low-Saturation color is moderately visible against a low-Contrast high-Value background, whereas the same color is more visible against a low-Contrast low-Value background.

A low-Value dark color on a medium-Value, low-Contrast background will look solid and clearly visible, whereas a low-Value color against a more highly

FIGURE 7.15   Low-Contrast background, with a Subdued Red-Violet that has been reduced in Saturation by 20%, White added by 35%, and Contrast reduced by 20%

FIGURE 7.16   Higher-Intensity and high-Contrast background, with the same Red-Violet variation from 7.15

FIGURE 7.17   A low-Saturation light background

FIGURE 7.18   A low-Saturation dark background

Saturated background will look even darker than it already is. A low-Value dark color will stand out clearly from a low-Contrast, high-Value background, whereas it will tend to blend into a low-Contrast, low-value background.

FIGURE 7.19   A low-Value garment against a low-Intensity background

Depending on the hue, a high-Value color will be visible on a medium-Value background and will stand out on a highly Saturated background. A high-Value color blends into a high-Value background and is most visible against a low-Value background.

FIGURE 7.20   A low-Value garment against a high-Saturation background

FIGURE 7.21   A low-Value garment against a light background

FIGURE 7.22   A low-Value garment against a dark background

FIGURE 7.23   A high-Value garment against a low-Saturation background

FIGURE 7.24   A high-Value garment against a high-Saturation background

FIGURE 7.25   A high-Value garment against a high-Value background

FIGURE 7.26 A high-Value garment against a low-Value background

A costume containing sharply contrasting Saturated hues will draw attention on a medium-Value background with low-Intensity colors, whereas the same costume will appear less visible on a highly Saturated background. A costume with contrasting Saturated hues will be clearly visible on a high-Value background, and it will stand out from a low-Value background with low contrasts **to the extent that the costume color contrasts are large enough** to see from the audience.

FIGURE 7.27 A high-Contrast garment against a low-Saturation background

FIGURE 7.28 A high-Contrast garment against a high-Saturation background

FIGURE 7.29 A high-Contrast garment against a low-Value background

FIGURE 7.30 A high-Contrast garment against a high-Value background

A costume with subtly contrasting Intensities may blend into a medium-Saturation or a low-Value background with low Contrasts. A costume with subtly contrasting Intensities will be visible on a high-Saturation or low-Value background with low contrasts, although the low-Contrast details within the costume may be lost against a background that has high contrast to the costume itself.

FIGURE 7.31   A low-Contrast garment against a low-Saturation background

FIGURE 7.32   A low-Contrast garment against a high-Saturation background

FIGURE 7.33   A low-Contrast garment against a high-Value background

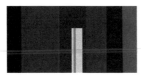

FIGURE 7.34   A low-Contrast garment against a low-Value background

Renderings

When rendering costumes, it is common to use White or pale paper in order to show off fabric colors. However, in most instances, the costumes will not be seen on a White set under clear White light. If possible, use a background color, whether in the paper itself or as an applied area of color on the paper, to represent the set color. This will create a preview of how the costumes will look on stage. Garments that seem very bright on a White paper background will usually look more subdued than one realizes on the stage, depending on the background and floor colors. See figures 7.35–7.40.

FIGURE 7.35   White background for renderings. All colors and details are clearly visible

FIGURE 7.36   High-value background. Colors and details are visible, although higher-Saturation colors and stronger contrasts are easier to see than Neutralized or Subdued colors

FIGURE 7.37 Medium-Value background. Low- to medium-Intensity costume colors tend to be absorbed, and details should have their contrasts intensified in order to be seen better onstage

FIGURE 7.38 Black background. Low-Value costume colors tend to be absorbed, whereas high-Value colors stand out more clearly

FIGURE 7.39   Sky-Blue background. Blue and medium-Intensity cool colors tend to be absorbed into this background

FIGURE 7.40   Saturated background

Color Value, Saturation, and Contrast in Combining Hues

Color Contrast refers to the difference between two or more hues in a composition. Color Value is the amount of lightness or darkness of a color, no matter what the base hue might be. Dark values (or Shades) have been blended with Black, Light values (or Tints) have been blended with White, and Tones have been blended with Grey. Color Saturation refers to the Intensity or Purity of a Hue. An Intense hue is a high-Saturation hue. A hue that has been mixed with Black, White, or Grey has had its Saturation lowered as well as its Value altered. Blending a hue with its complement will reduce its Saturation by Neutralizing it, and a hue blended with another hue in order to adjust the base hue can be said to have been Subdued to create a lower-Saturation color. Relative color **Saturations and Values will affect the visual Contrasts within a color scheme**.

Soft Contrast

Soft-Contrast combinations have colors of **similar Values** of darkness or lightness, whether the hues themselves are inherently Dark, Medium, or Light. Soft contrasts are also created with groups of a similar Saturation, often Neutralized or Subdued. Softly contrasting hues create a unified appearance. Many Categories of colors (see Chapter 5, Figures 5.17–5.34) have Soft Contrasts within the grouping because the category has a similar level of Saturation or Value that unites the colors in the first place. Use colors within a color Category for a softly contrasting effect.

Examples of Soft Contrasts within color combinations include:

Cream, Beige, pale Taupe – Light Neutrals	Peach, pale Yellow, soft Aqua – Pastel, or high-Value, soft, light, colors
Pale Pastel Pink, light Mauve, pale Blue – Pastels and Subdued high-Value colors	Peach, Mint, Lavender – Pastel to Medium colors
Mint, Aqua, pale Blue – Pastel to Medium colors	Medium Grey and dulled Pastels – High- to medium-value Tones and Subdued colors
Lavender, Soft Rose, Pale Blue-Grey – Subdued tones (Grey added)	Mauve, dull Blue-Grey, soft Camel Tan – Medium Subdued colors
Grey, Taupe, dull Tan – Medium Neutrals	Ruby Red, Emerald, Sapphire, Amethyst – Jewel tones
Navy, Forest Green, Burgundy – Neutralized dark colors	Navy, Deep Red, Brown – Dark, Deep colors
Black, Charcoal Grey, dark Brown – Dark Neutrals	Plum, Charcoal, Black – Deep Color plus Dark Neutrals

Medium Contrast

Medium-Contrast combinations can be created with different **Values that are one grouping away from each other**, such as a Light color with a Medium color or a Medium color with a Dark color, **or with different Saturation levels**, such as low- with medium-, or medium- with high-Saturation colors based on the Color Categories described in Chapter 5. Medium contrasts are a good starting point for successfully combining colors.

Combinations with medium contrasts include:

- Light plus Medium colors:

Soft Yellow, Pale Grey, Medium Sea Foam Green	Cream, Yellow, Sea Green,
Off White, Yellow, Coral	Off White, Yellow, Soft Red
White, Grey Green, Peach	Taupe, Soft Red, Beige
Beige, Celery Green, Medium Brick Red	Olive Green, medium Browned Red, Beige
Buff, Rose, Turquoise	Cream, Medium Blue, Dull Brick Red
Tan, Rust, Pale Olive	Beige, Warm Taupe, softened Red-Violet
Beige, softened Red-Violet, Blue-Green	Pastels plus Medium colors
Light Neutrals plus Medium Neutrals	Light Neutrals plus Subdued colors

- Saturated Pure or Neon colors, plus one or more Light or Medium colors:

Lime Green, Olive Drab, Blue-Grey	Magenta, French Blue, Pale Greyed Lavender
Magenta, Grey, Light Pink	Bright Magenta, Deep Teal, Clay Red-Brown
Saturated Red, Golden Tan, Olive Green	Bright Yellow, Aqua, Lavender
Magenta, Golden Tan, Grass Green	Medium Blue, Magenta, Dark Plum
Neon colors plus Pastels	Neon colors plus Light Neutrals
Saturated colors plus Medium colors	Saturated colors plus Medium Neutrals

- Medium plus Dark colors:

Peachy Tan, Dark Taupe, Chocolate Brown	Chocolate, Taupe, Grey Green
Coral, Charcoal, Medium Grey	Medium Blue, Clay, Chocolate
Deep Storm Cloud Blue, Clay, Butter Yellow	Red, Grey, Navy
Dark Blue-Grey, Clay, Olive drab	Teal, Charcoal, subdued Blue-Grey
Charcoal, Medium Blue, Warm Brown	Rust, Medium Blue, Charcoal
Olive Green, Purple, Charcoal, Orange accents	Navy Blue, Medium Brown, Warm Tan

Blue-Purple, Grey, Red	Medium Turquoise, Greyed Lavender, Deep Warm Brown
Red, Medium Tan, Chocolate	Teal, Olive, Deep Warm Brown
Medium Greyed Teal, Olive Green, Deep Blue-Purple	Bright Teal, Rust, Charcoal
Chocolate, Teal, Medium Grey	Camel Tan, Medium Brown, Navy
Red Brown, Grey Blue, Charcoal	Clay, Olive, Brown
Purple Black, Mauve, Medium Aqua	Medium Neutrals plus Jewel Tones
Medium Neutrals plus Deep Colors	Medium colors plus Dark Neutrals
Medium Neutrals plus Dark Neutrals	Ochre Gold, Dark Red, Aqua

Bold Contrast

Bold Contrast combinations combine Light with Dark Values or strong contrasts of Saturated hues that, when used together, will create a bold color scheme. Opposite colors on the color wheel at full Saturation, such as Red and Green, Orange and Blue, or Purple and Yellow, have the most contrast. These strong contrasts can add excitement to a composition, but can also be more difficult to blend attractively.

The greater the color Contrast in a costume, the more formal the effect. For example, a Black suit with a White blouse will appear more formal than a medium Blue suit with a pale Blue-Grey blouse. A very strong color contrast can also create a severe effect.

Bold color contrasts will call attention to a character, or to a section of the actor's figure. Bold contrasts tend to stop the eye at the edges where two colors meet and can visually subdivide a figure into smaller, usually horizontal, sections because of the lines created at the edges of colors. This should be considered carefully in relation to the actor's figure and the period effect that you are trying to create. Therefore, use bold color contrasts thoughtfully on stage.

Bold color contrasts include:

- Saturated colors in combination:

Clear red, Lemon Yellow, Hot Pink, Turquoise, White, Purple, Bright Green	Gold, Bright Yellow, Fire Engine Red, Cream, Lime Green, Royal Blue, Orange
Primary Red, Blue, Yellow	Bright Yellow, Magenta, Bright Teal
Orange, Magenta, Royal Blue	Lime, Magenta, Purple
Lime, Teal, Purple	Gold, Teal, Purple
Blue-Purple, Gold, Magenta	Teal, Magenta, Purple
Lime, Bright Aqua, Purple	Neon colors
Advancing colors	Saturated colors

- Combinations of Dark plus Light Values, including some with Medium tones added:

Pale Butter Yellow, Cream, Burgundy	Blue-Grey, Pale Linen, Charcoal
Cream, Charcoal, Deep Rust	Cream, Rusty Brown, Chocolate
Off-White, Saturated Blue, Black	Cream, Dark Grey-Blue, Charcoal Grey
Peach, Deep Blue-Grey, Cream	Peach, Warm Deep Brown, Cream
Off White, Coffee, Charcoal	Storm cloud Blue, Pale Lavender, Dark Plum
Blued Green, Rust, Black, Buttercream	Olive drab, Deep Burgundy, Cream
Turquoise Blue, Deep Olive drab, White	Olive drab, Dark Greyed Navy, Off-White
Dark Teal, Taupe, White, Black	Turquoise Blue, Deep Brown, Cream
Dark Red, Charcoal, Off-White	Camel, Pale Taupe, Black
Browned Deep Purple, Taupe, Celery Green	Dark Grey Green, Medium Warm Brown, Pale Taupe
Greyed Aqua, Ochre Gold, Burgundy, Beige	Olive, Camel, Medium Blue, Black, White
Dark Teal, Purple, Pale Mint Green	Warm Taupe, Red, Off-White, Black
Camel, Dark Greyed Aqua, Dark Red	Dark Brick Red, Greyed Pale Green, Medium Blue
Red, Khaki, Black	Purple, Warm Taupe, Beige, Green
Olive drab, Plum, Cream, Warm Black	Dark Red, Cream, Dark Brown
Black, White, Khaki	Black, White, Blue-Grey
Rose, Black, Grey	Olive, Black, White
Black, Red, White, Pale Grey	White, Black

On a related note, when considering color contrasts, remember that you may need to photograph your work for later professional use. Although eventual photos should not be the sole consideration when creating a color scheme, a very highly contrasting color scheme is difficult to photograph well, especially if costumes contain very dark colors or blacks along with whites or very pale colors. Extreme value contrasts will confuse the camera in terms of selecting the correct exposure or focus. It is difficult to get clear, crisp, accurate color images when the stage lighting is dim and the costumes have large areas of extreme contrasts. For that reason, use contrasts on stage a little more thoughtfully than you might use them in real life, so that the camera can record them correctly. A medium to medium-high contrast may be easier to record than a very high-contrast combination.

Using Contrasts in Value and Saturation as a Method of Creating a Color Scheme

One can combine almost any group of hues by reducing the Saturation of most of the hues in the grouping in order to reduce their inherent contrast. Two colors, combined with a light or medium Neutral, make a workable color scheme. Use one color as the Dominant color in terms of its size or intensity in a costume and the second color in a smaller area or as a less-intense Supporting color. For an even less-contrasting effect, choose the same color Value grouping for most of the garments in a costume, or choose tints and shades of a single hue. Different hues of the same Value in a single costume or a Monochromatic (tints and shades of a single hue) color combination will help elongate the figure because the low contrast does not visually break the figure into smaller horizontal subsections.

Darker colors are more formal, Lighter pastels are sweeter and more casual, Bright colors are bolder, Medium colors are unthreatening, and Greyed or Neutralized colors may appear either refined or dull, depending on how they look against an actor's coloring, the set, and the other costumes onstage.

Below are some combinations of color categories, based on Values and Saturation. For a fuller discussion of Color Categories and for examples of the specific colors in each general category, refer to Chapter 5.

- Dark Neutral, Light Neutral, Saturated Color
- Dark Neutral, Light Neutral, Dark Color
- Dark Color, Light Neutral, Saturated Color
- Dark Color, Medium Neutral, Dark Neutral
- Medium Color, Saturated Color, Dark Neutral, Light Neutral
- Saturated Color, Dark Neutral, Light Neutral
- Saturated Color, Dark Neutral, Medium Neutral
- Jewel tone, Dark Neutral, Medium Neutral
- Dark Neutral, Light color, Saturated color
- Dark Neutral, Jewel tone, Medium Neutral
- Dark Neutral, Dark Color, White
- Dark Neutral, Medium Neutral, Light Color.

Any of the combinations listed in this chapter can be a starting point for a costume color scheme, either for a single costume or for an entire production. Take one of these combinations and use any of the ways of organizing colors discussed in Chapter 5. Color values and contrasts may also be used to indicate characters and relationships; refer to Chapter 11 for an expanded discussion of how color can express characters.

8

COLOR WITH PATTERN AND TEXTURE

Color schemes may be extended and diversified with prints, surface patterns, and fabric textures. Patterns and textures can add the visual interest that makes a restricted color scheme work for a large number of costumes, without repeating the same colors in the same type of garments over and over again. For example, in a Red/White/Blue color scheme where men are wearing solid-colored justacorps coats, if there are more than than three men onstage, at least two men of the men will be in the same color justacorps coat. This is also true for a monochromatic color scheme, in which tints and shades of color may vary, but all the characters are essentially wearing the same hue. Solid colors in the same textures throughout a composition create a stylized and clearly "defined" color scheme; adding patterns and a variety of textures will create a more naturalistic effect, even when working with a limited color scheme, and will allow the garments to appear more varied because of the break-up of colors that a surface pattern will create.

Pattern

Print and woven-in patterns are a way of introducing visual texture into costumes. Stripes, Plaids, Houndstooth Checks, Gingham, Herringbone, Ditsy prints such as Dots or tiny Flower Buds or other small repeated motifs, Baroque Arabesques, Ogee patterns, Large Florals, Geometrics, Paisleys, Ikats, Jacquards, Lattices, Argyles, Trellises, Scrolls, Animal Prints, Toile, Border prints, and Chevrons are samples of the types of prints that may be used in costumes.

Patterns will give different textural effects depending on the shapes and spacing involved in the pattern itself. Closely spaced patterns can give a busy or complex effect. If the motifs are very small, the pattern may appear more as a soft texture than as a distinct pattern. Such a print may then work as a background for a larger contrasting print elsewhere on the garment. Small patterns seem more delicate, but can be fussy or indistinct. Patterns with widely spaced motifs will have a more formal, elegant effect, although, if the pattern is made up of widely spaced small motifs, it will create a dotted effect.

A pattern will draw attention to the area of the body on which it is placed. This can be used to draw attention to the face or towards some parts of the figure and away from others. Look carefully at prints to make sure that the patterns do not fall on parts of the body that you do not want to emphasize. Large patterns are bold, can draw focus to an area, and may even seem to make an area seem larger. Avoid putting large round prints directly over the breasts, the strongest color or shapes in the pattern at the groin, or a contrasting horizontal stripe at the derriere or bust.

Prints should incorporate at least two of the chosen hues in a color scheme or a Saturated version of one of the chosen hues plus a Neutral. When coordinating a solid color with a pattern, you can choose the Dominant, Supporting, or Accent color (see Chapter 5) from the print for your solid color garment. Make sure the color you have chosen is visible in the print from a distance.

When choosing printed patterns, be sure to look at them from at least 6 feet away – or squint your eyes – in order to see whether they become directional or create an awkward texture at a distance. For example, a small print might separate visually into horizontal blocks at a distance, which generally should be avoided if a more vertical appearance is intended for the characters.

Carefully evaluate the overall balance of a print versus the solid colors in a costume. For example, use a Dark or Neutral color in a jacket to coordinate with a patterned shirt for an elegant effect. The bolder the print, the harder it is to make it look elegant in a costume, and so pairing a bold print with a dark solid color will make the bold print less assertive. If a print is very striking, it will draw focus and may overwhelm the rest of the costume. On the other hand, stripes are an elegant way to use color in a print and can be a good way to introduce pattern into a costume, even for a designer who is unsure about using prints.

The fabric texture can affect the mood of a costume as well as the balance of solid colors as compared with surface patterns. For example, a cotton print shirt that is mostly Blue with Grey and White accents will be complemented by a Grey cotton twill trouser for a business casual look or by a White denim pant for a more casual look. For a more formal look, use the dominant Blue color from the print for a wool

FIGURE 8.1   Blue, Grey, and White, using diamond and stripe patterns

trouser. The print will unite two separate solid colors used elsewhere in the outfit, such as a Grey jacket and Blue trouser with the print in the example in Figure 8.1.

Two patterns may be combined with solid garments. To be successful in this, avoid using two large patterns that will fight one another. Instead, choose a Dominant print to mix with a Supporting or Accent print of different sizes and/or level of boldness. In this case, use one large and widely spaced pattern with a smaller pattern that may read as a surface texture rather than as a defined print. See Figure 8.1.

FIGURE 8.2   A "loose" floral print without formal repeats. This pattern combines will with figure 8.3

FIGURE 8.3   Small patterns will read as a subtle texture rather than as a defined print. Choose one of the colors in the dominant print (Figure 8.2) as the main color in the supporting pattern

A floral pattern can be used together with a stripe, open plaid, lattice, or other linear pattern if the sizes of the two patterns are different, because the ordered stripe, plaid, lattice, or linear pattern gives visual structure to the looser, rounded floral print. In this type of combination, the linear patterns act as a "trellis" for the floral and adds visual order to the floral, while the floral gives energy to the crisp geometric pattern. Make sure that the colors of the two different prints are chosen to be as similar as possible so that they will coordinate, or choose an important color from the floral print to repeat in the linear prints.

Custom-printed fabrics are becoming increasingly available from a number of online companies. Although the range of available fabrics is limited and tends to be more weighted towards synthetic than natural fibers, custom-printed fabrics can be a great way to get exactly the colors and motifs that a designer needs to pull a color scheme together. Some custom printing services start with predesigned

FIGURE 8.4 Aqua loose floral pattern

FIGURE 8.5 Aqua stripes Because this sample shares the same colors as figure 8.4, the two patterns would combine harmoniously

FIGURE 8.6 Loose floral pattern. Combine this pattern with the stripe in figure 8.7 to create visual interest

FIGURE 8.7 Green stripes

patterns that can be customized in terms of color. Other services allow a designer to upload an image and to adjust color, or to use ready-made patterns in set colors. The downsides here are a reasonably expensive price point, limited range of fabric types, the technical difficulties of designing the fabrics, and the time lag between ordering the fabric and receiving it. However, as this type of resource is more widely used, it may become easier to use and a more convenient option for many designers.

Some lucky costume shops may have the capability of printing or painting their own fabrics in-house. There can be a steep learning curve and significant start-up costs for materials and equipment. However, a university or design program that has made the investment towards allowing designers to create their own fabric patterns offers a wonderful resource to its students!

Texture and Color

The textures of fabric will affect perceived color. Glowing silk charmeuse, rich rayon velvets versus matte cotton velveteen, smooth cotton broadcloth shirting, sturdy cotton denim and twill, ribbed corduroy, fluid rayon jersey, napped wool flannel, nubby linen, soft sweater knit, and pearly cotton/rayon bengaline are examples of the many fabric textures that may be used onstage.

Shiny fabrics will draw focus onstage and will display more of the light-to-dark range of a hue because of the sheen in highlighted areas. Silk charmeuse is a satin-weave fabric with a satisfying glow that highlights the curves of the wearer's body. Colors in shiny fabrics will tend to look somewhat bolder on stage because they catch the eye more than flat textures.

A twill or satin weave, or a more expensive grade of cotton, linen, or wool fabric, will produce a slight sheen because, in this case, the fibers are longer and finer than the standard short fibers in a cheaper version of the same fabric or in a flat weave. Fabrics with a slight sheen have some of the aspects of shiny textures discussed above, which should be considered in combination with the other textures onstage. They can appear subtle and tasteful, as well as interesting, and tend to draw more focus than the same type of fabric in a flat texture. Extra-fine shirting cotton, cotton twills, linen twill weaves, and wool gabardines are useful examples of these types of fabrics.

Plain-weave cottons, linens, denims, knits, and wools often look flat. This may be a positive attribute, as the flat texture can make colors easier to combine because the surface texture is not calling for attention. In some cases, the plain-weave fabric may visually recede compared with more visually lively textures onstage. The color on a plain-weave fabric will appear true to the color that was intended.

Napped-surface fabrics have a richer, deeper color and appear more formal. Silk-and-rayon-blend velvet has more sheen and richness than the same color of cotton velveteen, but both will have a rich texture. Because velvet is harder to sew and to alter than cotton velveteen and is much more expensive, many designers use the velveteen option, except for Black, which is never as rich in velveteen as in velvet. Napped corduroy also takes color well and can be a cheaper alternative to velveteen when using feather-wale corduroy for a large-cast show. Brushed fabrics such as wool flannel or cotton flannelette have a slightly raised nap. In this case, the very short brushed surface hairs add a slightly pale "frost" to the base hue.

Dyed Color Tests

The same color will appear different on a variety of fabric fibers and surface textures. Samples of identical colors on a range of fabrics, including velvet, a jacquard weave cotton/rayon bengaline that creates a tonal pattern, and plain weave cottons are shown in Figures 8.8–8.11.

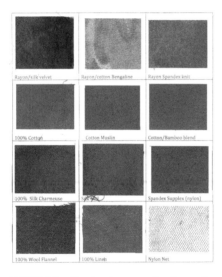

FIGURE 8.8   Scarlet dye tests, dyed together to show variations in the colors based on how different fabric textures and fiber contents take color

Results

As one can see, getting an even result when dyeing fabrics can be a challenge! (The samples in this case appear not to have been stirred consistently while they were being dyed and did not have enough space in the container to allow dye to spread evenly throughout the fabric.) The samples **are** useful for showing a variety of tints and shades available from a particular dye recipe, but a length of fabric intended for a costume would need to be dyed much more slowly, in a large container, using the correct mordants, and with steady stirring throughout the process.

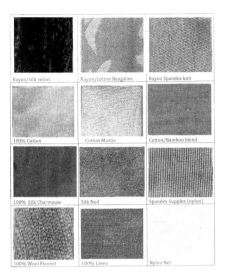

FIGURE 8.9 Blue dye tests, showing variations in the colors based on different fabric textures and fiber contents

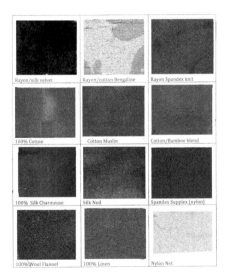

FIGURE 8.10 Purple dye tests, showing variations in the colors based on different fabric textures and fiber contents

All the textiles in Figures 8.8–8.11 were dyed together, with the same color mixture, and were in the water for the same amount of time, but the fiber content and surface texture of different fabrics affect how the color takes on the fabric and how the color is perceived.

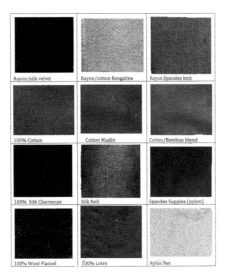

FIGURE 8.11   Black dye tests, showing variations in the colors based on different fabric textures and fiber contents

The silk/rayon blend velvet consistently took dye the most deeply, partially because silk fibers are very accepting of dye and partly because the napped velvet texture adds depth to each color.

Wool also takes dye well. As silk and wool are both protein fibers, they absorb dye readily.

Nylon takes dye quickly but takes time to build a deep color. However, it is best to build that color slowly or the nylon will get streaks. This is a good tip if you decide to dye tights for a show to add more color – take a little time in the process to get a smooth and consistent result. Nylon net takes dye quicky, but its sheer texture creates a "veil" of color rather than a solid impression.

Cotton accepts dye easily up to a point, but also has a tendency to lose color in the wash. Rayon takes dye better than cotton. The rayon/cotton blend Bengaline pictured in the figures has a woven-in jacquard pattern, and the pattern is revealed by the variations of the dye on that surface.

Linen takes dye reasonably well if it is dyed slowly. The natural greyish color of linen tends to tone down whatever color the fabric is being dyed.

Textures combined with colors can play off one another to create unity or variety within a costume. In terms of texture, strike a balance between contrast and repetition, rough and smooth. Too much contrast is jarring, too much repetition is boring. If the textures of an outfit are varied or strikingly contrasted, keep the colors closely related and use low contrasts of color values. If the fabric textures are similar and simple, use more differentiation in color or surface pattern to create variety between characters.

Textures also help define characters. Rough textures and mottled surface patterns tend to be used for people who have a relationship with the natural world, whether peasants, farmers, or eco-friendly people in nubby linen. Plain textures and solid colors can be used for refined and tidy characters. Shiny textures may indicate a range of characters, from refined and tasteful characters in glowing silks to loud characters in very shiny gold lamé. Finally, plush and napped fabrics appear cozy and luxurious, which adds an inviting element to a character.

9

COLOR FROM AN INSPIRATION SOURCE

If combining colors proves difficult on its own, artwork and photographs are great starting points for creating a color scheme. Analyzing artworks such as well-known paintings, decorative sources such as fabric prints or ceramics, or interior designs can provide a starting point from which to extract colors. Magazines and department store displays, whether of interior designs, housewares, accessories, or clothing, tend to be created by visually talented designers, so use their expertise for your own inspiration. Catalogues and advertisements may also be good sources of color schemes.

Creating a Color Scheme Based on a Visual Source

If you find a visual source that feels right for a production, note the relationships of colors and of neutrals, the use of stronger colors as accents, and how the colors lead your eye to a focal point. For costumes, these elements can be translated into garment colors and accents that lead the viewer's eye to the actor's face.

Then, reproduce the major colors from the source by using paint chips, or color media such as watercolors or markers on a blank page. Be sure to duplicate the Saturation/Intensity and Value of each hue. Take note of the **Proportion** of each color in the source in order to fully replicate the mood of the original art-work. Many designers skip this step and end up with costume colors that do not align with the color source. Of course, the audience will not necessarily be aware of the original color source and will, therefore, not be able to judge whether the designer has successfully reproduced the source or not. However, if the entire design team is using the same color source, it is helpful if each designer maintains some fidelity to the source.

Once the colors have been reproduced, cut the paint chips or the colored areas you have created into separate pieces that can be moved around to experiment with color combinations. If you are using the colors on a computer screen, you can capture areas of color to create new areas as starting points. Use the hues in combinations to start building the color scheme.

This method will educate the designer's eye to how different colors can combine well, how small areas of Accent colors will enliven a color scheme, and how varying proportions of the colors can express different characters.

The steps to develop a color scheme, based on a variety starting points are:

- Select a color source.
- Pull out all the colors with paint chips, watercolor paint, color pencils, markers, fabric swatches, on a computer screen, or with other media.
- Reproduce the proportions of each color from the color source.
- Separate the color samples into movable pieces.
- Move the colors around to make combinations.
- Record any combinations that seem to work for the production, by photos, photocopying, or by securing the chips together and setting them aside for future use.
- Assign color combinations to major characters. Factor in the characters' personalities, function in the play, and any special actions or occasions in the script.
- Refine and adapt the most promising combinations to express supporting characters and their relationships to the main character(s).
- Arrange the colors in each combination to reflect **where the colors will be placed on each costume**. For example, if the character wears a suit, arrange the color chips to reflect the long vertical edges of a suit jacket and skirt or trousers, with a smaller area of the shirt or blouse beneath, along with any accent colors that may be used for the costume.

Starting with a simple photo, figures 9.1-9.6 show some steps to follow in extracting the colors.

Extract the colors from the inspiration source, in this case by using paint sample chips. The lens flare of the original photo was included as a color swatch. The samples were scanned as a starting point, then adjusted to reflect smaller areas that weren't noticed before the initial scan.

Altering the colors to match the source is a good way to really **see** the hues in terms of Saturation, Value, and Temperature. This will also be helpful later, if any fabric needs to be tinted to adjust the colors. Different designers may get slightly different results from the same original source owing to differences in how individuals perceive color. Adjusting the color proportions is very valuable in forcing a designer to analyze the specific colors in the inspiration source.

When creating the color combinations in Figure 9.6, the color areas were used in much the same proportions as the original source (Figure 9.1) and the finished color proportion collage (Figure 9.4). Start with the major, large areas of color

FIGURE 9.1 Original inspiration photograph: London spiral

FIGURE 9.2 Color scan of paint samples used to start the process of capturing the colors in Figure 9.1. Other designers may use other methods for representing colors from the original source, such as painting their own color samples or by building colors on a computer

and then refine each combination with a Supporting color or two drawn from the original source. Finish up by using Accents to add interest and to start building visual relationships.

To my eye, the colors in this exercise suggest dark suits and subdued garments, with the smaller areas of brighter colors available to be used as accents within the costume. The combinations were put together with the 1920s in mind, as the original photograph was taken as inspiration for a production of *Machinal* based in the 1920s. The color combinations from Figure 9.6 allowed the designs in Figure 9.7 to be quickly filled in, as the major color decisions were made while organizing the colors and their proportions.

As a group, these color combinations may be useful for a unified chorus. For the main characters in a production, consider giving them more of the accent colors, while using less of the accents for the chorus. Or, use more distinct Contrasts or color Saturations, or add some of the spiral motif of the staircase seen in the source photo in order to make the main characters stand out in the crowd. Once the strongest color combinations are chosen for the main characters,

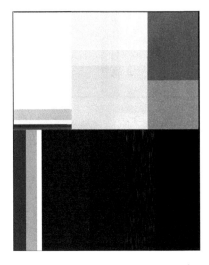

FIGURE 9.4 Color proportions from Figure 9.2 are adjusted to more accurately represent the proportions in Figure 9.1

FIGURE 9.3 Color scans from Figure 9.2 are adjusted to more accurately represent the colors in Figure 9.1

the designer can diffuse the remaining colors throughout the costumes that the supporting characters will wear. You can see colors repeated in the combinations above as they were composed.

Going back to the color inspiration source shown earlier in this chapter (Figure 9.1), there is a clear focal point at the center of the picture, where the spiral staircase leads to the top landing. This is supplemented by a contrast of the dark landing at the center point and the lighter surrounding walls immediately surrounding the landing. The open squares of the support trusses also lead the eye to the central focal point. All of these are great ideas to keep in mind as the costumes are developed, in order to reinforce the focal point of the actors' faces. The squared accents of the original source are mimicked in the color contrasts that are indicated in the final color combinations in Figures 9.6 and 9.7.

Working with the Design Team

When sharing color sources with the Scenic and Lighting designers, be sure to take time to collaborate over which design areas will use which colors as their palette. If the color source was brought in by the director and is intended to be the cornerstone of the designs, it is especially important to be clear about how each design area will interpret the color source. If the colors onstage are **too** harmonious, the costumes will be lost on the larger set. In this case, use higher Saturation

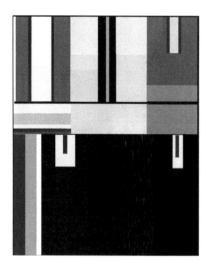 

FIGURE 9.5 Color combinations being tried out by moving areas of color around

FIGURE 9.6 Color combinations complete. The illustration represents three women's 1920s costumes with hats on the upper register, and three men's costumes with hats on the lower register.

versions of the colors from the source and more of the accent colors for the costumes, to be bolder than the set. If the Lighting designer is using the color source, ask them about what sort of light they are envisioning. Using the color source at the start of this chapter, the light could be very clear White, slightly Grey and frosted, or more Greyed and murky, depending on which area of the source the designer is inspired by. It is likely that all three of these lighting choices could be made at various points in the production.

If the color source has been selected by the costume designer for use on the costumes, it is helpful for the other designers to see the costumes' color direction. However, be careful that the other designers do not get **so** inspired by your colors that they use them, resulting in costumes that get lost on the stage! In this case, consider offering to give the other designers a copy of your inspiration, but **reduce the color intensity in the copies** (Figure 9.8), **while you make yourself a copy with intensified versions of the colors** as your guide (Figure 9.9).

Adding Red or other Saturated color accents is helpful for making actors stand out from the scenery if the set and costume colors are so similar that the costumes are hard to see (Figure 9.10).

FIGURE 9.7 1920s costumes based on the color scheme in Figure 9.6

Inspiration Color Sources and Proportional Colors

Compare the original inspiration images in Figures 9.11, 9.13, and 9.15 with the scanned colors that are arranged in proportions. These are good starting points for assembling combinations and costume colors. The process of pulling color out of a source is a valuable exercise for sharpening a designer's ability to really see color and to reproduce it. Building the proportional relationships reveals the structure of the source.

For a designer, a color inspiration source can be an invaluable starting point. It can provide a way to communicate with the director and other designers about the mood and world of the production. It can also limit the number of colors under consideration when starting to choose colors for each costume. Overall, the color source can provide a framework within which to work while designing.

Many works of art have an inherent coherence that can be extracted through careful observation of the exact Value and Temperature of the colors, of how the colors are arranged together, of the proportions of the colors, and of how the viewer's eye moves around the composition to a focal point. Use these observations as is helpful to your design and color process. The audience may never see the inspiration source and, thus, will not judge a designer on whether they perfectly captured the source or not. However, the source will provide a good starting point for color decisions.

FIGURE 9.8   Image from Figure 9.1 with reduced color Intensity

FIGURE 9.9   Image from Figure 9.1 with increased color Intensity

FIGURE 9.10   Image from Figure 9.9 with added Accents

FIGURE 9.11 Lyon rooftops

FIGURE 9.12 Rooftop colors

FIGURE 9.13 Indiana trees

FIGURE 9.14 Indiana tree colors

FIGURE 9.15 Hampton Court garden

FIGURE 9.16 Hampton Court garden colors

10

COLOR SCHEMES FROM WHAT IS AVAILABLE

Being able to develop a costume color scheme completely from the script and the director's concept is a luxury. Usually, the costume design needs to incorporate costumes from stock – the theatre's own stock and what is available to rent or borrow – what is available to purchase, and whatever appropriate fabric types are available for sale. Many of us may not have enough time, skilled labor, or budget to create an entire show from scratch. Existing garments and available materials will need to be factored into the design.

Often, a designer must coordinate a group of garments from a variety of sources. Pulled, rented, and restyled garments may share the stage with a number of specifically purchased garments and/or built costumes. Knowing how to take a disparate group of items and create a color scheme is invaluable for a working designer. The resulting color scheme does not necessarily need to be obvious to the audience; for a naturalistic effect, the colors need only to help the audience understand the characters and their relationships.

Here are some approaches to working with available elements, starting with an overall method and then discussing specific methods for creating a color scheme with pulled garments or in the fabric or retail store.

Approach I: Identify What You Already Have and What You Can Gather

As soon as actors' measurements are available, begin to pull costume options from the theatre stock and from any other costume sources that are available from which to borrow or rent. Check the garment measurements against actors' measurements to identify which garments are good options for the show.

1. Try the garments on dress forms if possible, in order to avoid falling in love with items that have no chance of being worn by a particular actor. It is helpful to take a group of appropriately sized dress forms into a quiet room and start to dress them, as it is useful to see the garments as a grouping and in combination with one another. This also helps save time in later fittings with actors. Very often, one can find a combination of garments that wasn't initially planned, in colors that work together. Take photos of any garments and combinations that seem to work and label which character and/or scene they will work for.

   Begin to create a clear and complete costume list of all the pieces that will be needed for the production, in order to get a sense of what the budget needs to be stretched to cover. This process helps define which garments will need to continue to be searched for, which will need to be built, and what the actual workload for the production will be. It may be more fun to build a lovely gown for the leading lady, but it may be more necessary to build costumes for some of the background characters or to purchase menswear if there are already good options for the leading lady in stock.

2. Begin to explore what materials will be available for the project at the same time that you are pulling garments from stock. The time period and style of the garments you are designing will limit the types of fabric that are appropriate. Budget constraints will also be a limit, particularly if the garments need a lot of yardage and the appropriate fabric has a high per-yard cost. Factor in the costs of interfacing, underlining and support fabrics, lining, and trim. The exterior garment fabric usually adds up to about 60% of the garment cost, with other materials taking up the rest of the per-costume budget. Once you consider appropriate fabric type, amount needed, availability (whether locally or online), and costs, the color choices may be much more limited than you expect.

   Because of this, try to purchase fabric with at least 50% natural fiber content so that the color can at least be adjusted, if not changed, through dyeing. As the color scheme develops during the search for garments and fabrics, it is helpful to be able to adjust and tone the fabric as needed. A good cotton twill or corduroy fabric can be used for period bodices, coats, vests, breeches, and other mid-weight garments. Silk habotai, also known as China silk, is great for flowy period shirts, scarves, lightweight blouses, and fluttery dresses. Cotton/rayon or cotton/acetate bengaline fabric is a useful choice for period gowns and fancy men's period coats or vests, comes in a variety of colors, and is also dyeable. As the color scheme develops during the search for actual garments to use, it is helpful to be able to adjust and tone any fabric as needed.

   If the fabric swatches you have gathered are dyeable and **if** you have the facilities and skill to dye fabrics, do some preliminary dye tests for possible color options. This can be done with 2 cups boiling water in clean 2-quart containers with ¼-teaspoon (this teaspoon should be **only** for dye tests and

never for food) total of powdered dye. Add ¼ teaspoon salt and 1 tablespoon vinegar. Stir in a wetted-and-wrung-out swatch of fabric, after the dye is thoroughly dissolved, and let sit in the solution for 20 minutes, stirring often. After rinsing the fabric, remember to safety-pin a label with the dye recipe onto the swatch if you are dyeing a number of colors. Let the swatch air-dry. Even if the color is not exactly what you hoped for, you may be on the way to your ideal color and you will find out whether the fabric is dye-able.

When gathering fabric swatches, look for fabrics that will:

a.   Be structurally appropriate for the time period and mood of the production.

b.   Be reasonable to work with for the time and skill level of the technicians available.

c.   Be affordable with the yardage needed for the garments in question.

d.   Be available in the desired color for the character **or** is able to be dyed to the right color in the time frame and with the skill and facilities available. This would necessitate dyeable fibers such as silk, cotton, wool, linen, rayon, or nylon.

e.   Have the right type of surface pattern for the period and look of the production **or** be able to be printed in the time frame and with the skill and facilities available.

As fabric stores have become sparse in many cities, online fabric stores are an increasingly important source. If you find fabric that looks promising in an online store, be sure to order a large swatch or the minimum amount of yardage available so that you can feel the texture and see the true color in person when deciding on which fabrics to purchase. Be sure to consider the amount of yardage available and whether the fabric is returnable if it is not used. Also, keep the shipping time in mind once you order fabric and be prepared for yardage to sell out in the time between when a swatch is ordered and it is delivered. You may have to gather several fabric options in order to find one that will work for the project and is available in the needed amount.

Custom-printed fabrics are becoming increasingly available from a number of online companies. If you are able to order custom-printed fabrics for a production, consider whether the available fabrics will follow the suitability guidelines for any other swatches or yardage, in addition to arriving in sufficient time to allow for construction to occur prior to fittings and first dress rehearsal.

3. Looking at the garments and fabrics you have gathered, a color scheme may begin to develop. Concentrate on two to three main hues along with Neutrals (such as White, Cream, Tan, Brown, Grey, and Black) and repeat the hues in variations of Saturation, surface pattern, and where the color will be positioned on the body to create a sense of unity between costumes.

If the budget does not allow building costumes for an entire production, a unifying color of fabric or trim may be added to existing garments, whether the garments are pulled, purchased, or rented. Sashes, belts, edging on necklines and sleeve ends, bindings on lapels, pocket squares, neckwear, and hat trims can be made from small amounts of fabric in one or more accent colors that will visually tie all the garments together.

Approach II: Designing in the Fabric Store

When one is purchasing or swatching fabrics, a great deal of the color scheme is developed in the fabric store itself. It can be overwhelming to pull together many different fabrics when shopping in person, particularly if the fabric store is in a different city from where you are based. If possible, it may be worth taking several trips to the store so that the fabric decisions can be made in a deliberative manner. However, although it is preferable to be able to swatch fabrics from a variety of sources and then take time to consider the options before making purchasing decisions, it is sometimes necessary to purchase fabrics in a single trip to a store or fabric district. In this situation, give yourself plenty of time that day and be willing to clean up after yourself, as moving fabric around will be part of the process. Here are some suggested steps for working in the store:

1. Gather all the fabric bolts that you like. If something appeals to you for the production but you had not planned to use that type of fabric, consider it anyway at this point. Be sure to check that there is enough yardage on the bolt (two layers around the cardboard center of a rectangular bolt represents approximately one yard), and that the fiber content is appropriate: for the production, for the ability to tint the fabric if needed, for actor comfort, and for the skill level of the costume shop. If the fabric doesn't fit those requirements, **don't choose it** unless you need to have a swatch for purposes of finding something better, but be sure to note that the particular swatch is for information only.

    Gather all the bolts that may work and eliminate anything that would be inappropriate.

2. Find a quiet corner of the store where you can work without being in the way of other people and where the light is adequate. Start by grouping the fabric bolts into like piles of colors and patterns, arranging the fabric in piles that work well together. The piles may be organized by similar colors, surface patterns, and fabric texture, or may represent different character groupings. Arrange the piles of like fabrics, gather more fabric to round out what has already been gathered, and then arrange in piles by character. Continue moving the bolts until you find color combinations that work for the characters and their relationships.

For an ensemble cast, try to "balance" the piles so that they have similar visual weights of color Intensity and Patterns. For a production that has a clear Main character, I arrange the fabric options for that character and then work outwards from there to illustrate the relationships between other characters. Make sure that the Main character stands out in this grouping, either with slightly more Saturated colors, or with colors that are at least somewhat different than any other characters' colors. Characters who need to work together onstage may be put in colors that coordinate or in the very same colors if the colors are repeated in different places on their costumes. There will often be several rounds of hunting for more fabric, adding and subtracting choices, and rearranging until a clear set of options emerges. Take photos of the piles so that you can recreate these compositions when you are designing the costumes.

Looking at the fabrics you have gathered, a color scheme may begin to develop. Concentrate on two to three main hues, along with neutrals, and repeat those in variations of intensity, pattern, and position on the body to create a sense of unity between costumes.

Be sure to **walk away from the fabrics and then look back at them** from a distance. Colors and textures that may be attractive at close range can look very different from the distances at which the audience will see them. Colors that are subtle and quiet up close can appear faded and dull at a distance, and patterns can appear either invisible or overwhelming. A color that is exciting by itself may overwhelm everything else and need to be eliminated from consideration, or it may inspire you to go back and look for additional colors to support the bold color. If the lighting in the store is dim, a flashlight will be helpful, or bring the fabric to a large window. It is important to see the actual fabric colors, both individually and in combination.

3. Bring the fabrics to the cutting counter and obtain swatches of the fabric if possible (which tend to be tiny and of limited quantity) or purchase the smallest amount possible of the fabrics that are the most interesting. If a free swatch of a printed fabric is available, be sure to take a photo of the fabric spread out on the cutting table. If no free swatches are available, and you must purchase every sample, it may be necessary to take individual photos of solid-color fabrics if you need to avoid purchasing those samples in order to keep your swatching costs down. However, when considering printed or textured fabrics, it makes sense to purchase 2" or ⅛ yard (whichever is the smallest amount available) in order to have a clearer record of the surface pattern. If you will be showing fabric options to a director, it is also useful to purchase a small amount of yardage, as a tiny swatch is generally so small that a director cannot really understand the fabric that you are proposing for a costume. In this case, a director will tend to gravitate to the fabric options that have the larger swatches or photos, whether or not the larger swatches are better options than any tiny free swatches.

Whether you take photos of individual fabrics, get small free swatches, or buy small pieces, at each store be sure to **record all of the information on each sample**, such as the fabric type, fiber content, width, cost per yard, care instructions, and how much yardage appears to be on the bolt, as well as the store in which it was found. If you will be placing an online or phone order at a later time, also be sure to record any identifying codes on the bolt so that you are sure that you receive the correct fabric in your shipment.

4. Make a master reference sheet of all the sampled fabrics after having shopped in the fabric store or group of stores. Label each sample with the information of fabric type and so on, including the store from which the fabric was obtained.

5. Cut a piece of the fabric from each sample so that there are mobile pieces as well as the reference page. Using the photos of the piles of fabric bolts as a guide, move the mobile fabric swatches around so that you can see the possible combinations for each built costume. If you are considering tinting fabrics, now is the time to make dye tests using the small pieces of purchased yardage.

Alternatively, purchase dyeable fabrics in bulk and do color tests first – if dyeing, you can create interesting and complex colors as long as you take the process slowly to avoid streaks. Silk, wools, cottons, and dancewear are all dyeable. However, be mindful if you dye much of the fabric or garments for a show, as having a lot of dyed garments will result in a show where handwashing and dry cleaning are the only ways to launder the costumes owing to the possibility of dye colors running in the wash.

Approach III: Designing in the Second-Hand or Retail Clothing Store

Prior to shopping, be sure to pull any costume options from the theatre's stock and check the sizes against actor measurements, in order to avoid purchasing garments that the theatre already owns. The process of shopping for garments and accessories is very similar to the process in the fabric store.

1. Gather everything that you are considering, after you have checked for size and whether the fabric content is appropriate in terms of actor comfort, ease of care, and time period. Also check the garments' price points and potential alterability. Double check that none of the garments have stains, sweat marks, tears, or other visible or structural flaws.

2. Find a quiet corner of the store where you can work without being in the way of other people and where the light is adequate. Start arranging the garments in groups that work well together. The groups may be organized by garment types, surface patterns, and fabric texture, or may represent

different characters or groupings. I tend to start with groups of types of garments, gather more garments to round out what has been gathered, and then arrange in groups of ensembles by character.

For a production that has a clear Main character, arrange the options for that character and then work outwards to illustrate the relationships between other characters. You may find that a color for the Main character that you had not planned emerges during this process, which may work beautifully for your production and shape the rest of your garment color choices. For an ensemble cast, balance the garment groups so that they have a similar visual weight of color Intensity and of surface texture and patterns.

There will often be several rounds of hunting for more garments, adding and subtracting choices, and rearranging until you have a set of viable costume options. Take photos of the garment groups you have created so that these compositions can be recreated when hanging the garments behind character rack tags in the costume shop. Finally, be sure to measure the key points of the garments and check against the body measurements of whomever you are considering assigning the garments.

3. Determine which garments to purchase so that actors can try them on. Be sure to check the store return policy. Most second-hand stores do not allow for returns, or will only allow returns for store credit within a short time period. Online purchases may be inexpensive and convenient, but are sometimes very difficult to return. Therefore, unless you are very sure you can use your purchases from these sources for the production, it can be more budget-friendly to purchase items at a local retail store that allows full cash returns for at least a month after the purchase date. If there are garments that you like but are not able to purchase at this point, take a photo for further reference. Be sure to note at which store each garment has been seen or purchased, so that you can find the garments when ready to purchase them, and so that any returns are more convenient.

4. In the costume shop, try the purchased garments on dress forms that are appropriately sized for each actor or on a rolling rack if dress forms are not available. Combine these garments with any pulled items in order to create ensembles that can later be tried on actors. Group the dress forms to represent all the major characters in each scene so that they may be seen in relation to one another. This will also allow for adding and subtracting colors to unify costumes and to clarify character relationships. Take photos to record this work and to study the relationships between the costumes for future reference while fitting the costumes.

Once you have gathered the available pulled garments, fabrics, and purchased garments, you may find that there is a commonality of colors that can be used to illustrate characters and mood for the production. Establish the colors for the main character(s), then add selected colors to create unity, express relationships, and establish the visual style.

No matter the combination of pulled, built, and/or borrowed costumes, color distribution should be carefully thought out in order to create overall unity. Consider potential fabric and garment choices against any blocks of colors that you know will be part of the color scheme. Make sure one color or closely related group of colors dominates the overall composition in terms of size, that there are contrasts of Values and Saturation, and that the colors repeat in the composition.

If you are using pulled items for the Main characters, determine the colors that they will be in and how those colors can be repeated for related characters. The colors taken from the Main characters' garments can be used for accessories, belts, binding, prints, neckties, pocket squares, hats, or garments for other characters. More discussion of how to use color to express characters and relationships can be found in the next chapter.

11

COLOR AND CHARACTERS

Costumes are an important element for expressing characters and their relationships so that the audience will understand them. A costume designer must look closely at each character and understand them on a variety of levels in order to express the character clearly.

Each character can be explored in several ways:

1. **As individuals**, characters can be defined in terms of personality over the arc of the play, mood at a particular moment in the play, age, wealth, sense of taste and fashion, gender identification, and sense of modesty, sensuality, and display.
2. **Each character exists within a larger social context, in relation to other characters** in their world. The audience may not be completely familiar with the time period or culture in which the play is set, but the costumes can help them understand how the characters function within that context. A character will have a level of status and respect within society, be a part of a social class based on education and family ties, have a certain amount of wealth and resources, possess power and control over other characters **or** exist under the control of others, act as part of a group with alliances and family ties, and function in relationships with romantic partners, friends, and/or antagonists.
3. **All characters have a structural function to help further the action and the themes of the script**. Characters may range from the Protagonist or Main character, whose journey we witness during the play, to the Antagonist or obstacle to the Main character's progress, to Supporting characters who help advance the actions and ideas, plus Comic Relief, the Voice of Reason, a Chorus or crowd that expresses societal values, and the Stock

Characters such as *commedia dell'arte* characters or traditional figures with specific actions and costumes in a particular society.

Start by determining the **Protagonist**, whose journey is followed in the play. The Protagonist may also be called the **Main** character. Then, decide which character is at the top of the social structure in the play, with a relationship with most of the other characters. I refer to this character as the **Apex** character, in the sense that this character is often the center of a web of relationships and also has the highest social status. The Apex character is often the same as the Main character, but this is not always the case. For example, Figaro in *The Marriage of Figaro* is the Title character and he is the Protagonist or Main character. However, Count Almaviva may be interpreted as the Apex character because he is the highest-status character, with an employer relationship to Figaro. Figaro acts as a disrupter and questioner of the social structure that Almaviva represents. Figaro is the Protagonist, and Almaviva is the Antagonist, albeit an Antagonist who is at the Apex of the social group onstage.

Although the Main character's name may be used as the title of the play, this is not always the case. In *Tartuffe*, the title character does not appear until Act 3, and he is an outlier from most of the other characters. Consider Monsieur Orgon, the father of the family, as the Apex character in *Tartuffe*, because all other characters have a clear familial, servant, or antagonistic relationship to him. In addition, Orgon is the character who grows and learns during the course of the play, making him the Protagonist, whereas Tartuffe himself becomes the Antagonist. In this case, color relationships could logically depict all the characters in relation to Orgon.

In *The Misanthrope*, the title character, Alceste, is at odds with every other character, including his love interest, Célimène. Célimène is a wealthy young widow at the apex of her small group of suitors, each of whom becomes an antagonist to Alceste in turn. In this case, the suitors and Célimène's maid could be in colors that relate to Célimène, while Alceste could be dressed in austere hues that put him outside of the group and of society at large, as he is an Antagonist to the rest of the world.

In all of these examples, the character relationships can be depicted with color. Costume colors will indicate characters and relationships through manipulation of the Intensity, Value, Temperature, Contrast, and combinations of colors. Although it might seem very mechanical to assign colors in this manner, unless the costume scheme is very obvious, the audience may not consciously be aware of it, and it can be extremely helpful for the audience to keep track of who is who in the play. This approach is especially useful in a play with many characters and tangled relationships. For an audience that is not used to hearing Shakespearean language or following an opera plot, being able to get a sense of the characters through color cues can be a valuable way to understand the story.

Let us explore characters, first as individuals and then as part of the web of relationships in a play, with notes on possible ways to **depict them through**

color. For more on the meaning of colors in different societies, refer to Appendix 1. For more on how to use these color variations in a color scheme, see Chapter 14.

Individual Characters and Their Aspects, with Ideas on Color Choices

Personality

- Exuberant characters may be illustrated with Light and Dark colors together, Primary colors, and vivid Contrasts.
- If a character is bold, consider high-Intensity colors such as Red or Orange.
- Balanced characters can use Light and Dark versions of a single hue, with an Accent color for interest.
- Very Neutralized and Greyed versions of colors may indicate withdrawn or boring characters.
- If a character is reliable and steady, consider a medium-Intensity color that is common to clothing, such as Blue. Blue tends to be seen as a sign of trust and fidelity in many cultures.
- For a character that is delicate or flighty, consider Pastels or high-Value colors, possibly in a print.
- If a character is eccentric, consider Saturated hues such as Purple for a modern-day production, or Complementary colors for a highly contrasted effect.

Age

- Pastel hues are commonly used for the young, especially children.
- Medium-value non-Neutralized colors work for young adults.
- Deeper and/or Greyed hues can indicate older characters, as Darker and Subdued colors suggest a steadier personality, more grounded-ness, and lessened vitality.

Sense of Taste and Fashion

- Refined and sophisticated characters may be indicated by medium-Value, somewhat Neutralized colors with medium Contrasts plus Light and Dark Accents.
- Fashionable characters may be costumed in the most fashionable colors of the time period in which the production is set, with at least one of the colors in the combination used with heightened Intensity. See Appendix 2 for fashionable colors for a range of time periods and cultures.
- Very sharp Contrasts or Neon versions of colors may indicate a loud or less-than-tasteful character.

Wealth, Status, and Power

- Saturated versions of a color may be used with Light Neutrals for wealthy characters, as these hues make it appear that the costume is new and that the character does not have to perform physical labor.
- More Neutralized or Browned colors may indicate poorer characters or laborers.
- Accents of the employer's color can be used in servants' costumes.

Gender

- In Europe and North America, males tended to wear the same amount or **more** color and accessories than females prior to around 1800, after the French Revolution. See Appendix 2, which shows how male color schemes start to differ from females' colors in the 19th century.
- In Europe and North America, females began to wear **more** color and accessories than males after 1800; males wore increasingly subdued colors in the 19th century and up to the middle of the 20th century.
- After the middle of the 20th century, color preferences are not as separated by gender as they had been since 1800, or as specific to different geographic areas for most daily wear garments. However, special-occasion clothing tends to maintain earlier color traditions for many societies.
- Some gendered color conventions, such as pale Pink for baby girls and pale Blue for baby boys, are relatively recent in European and North American cultures and are not universal even now. Be aware of what the gendered color meanings may be for your audience.

Once you have analyzed the characters with the list above and have determined the Main character, choose a signature color for the Main character. This color can be adapted to illustrate various characters and their relationships to the Main character through different color Values and Saturation or Purity. Based on their relationships to the Main character, the size of the area that the main character's color covers can be varied for different characters and costumes. For example, if the Main character is costumed in a full-length garment of a particular color, such as a Blue gown or suit, closely related characters may repeat the same color in a smaller garment, such as a jacket, vest, blouse, or shirt.

In this example, the Main character's signature color is varied to indicate character relationships. However, if you do not intend to create a noticeable color scheme, choose colors that have **similar** Intensity and Value to link the Main character and their allies.

A useful method to illustrate character relationships is to create a collage of colors and images for the play, laid out so that the colors and images are grouped to mirror the relationships. For example, the Main character might be represented by Green and the image of a wrought-iron gate, placed at the center of the collage. Characters who need to relate to the Main character could then be symbolized by colors that are related to or are analogous to Green, and by images that work with the image of a wrought-iron gate. A designer can build out from the central images and colors to show variations of these themes as colors and motifs diffuse outwards to supporting characters. This collage can be a private tool for a costume designer to map out relationships and may or may not be shared with the director and other designers. The collage can also be built as a group project with the design team as the show concept is developed.

Character Relationships

The Main character's color may be diffused to other characters to indicate relationships. Start with the Main character and work outwards.

1. Love interests or partners may repeat the Main character's color or use a version of that color, with the color placed in a different position on the body. For example, a couple may have one character in a Purple coat and the other character in Purple breeches or a skirt. Or, the main color may be used in a smaller area but in a higher-Intensity version on the love interest. Exactly matching colors in the same body position on two characters may be interpreted as "too match-y," but there are times when this effect may be exactly what is needed.

2. Close associates: Friends and partners may be in darker shades or lighter tints of the Main character's color, in smaller amounts of the color, or in colors that are Analogous (next to one another on the color wheel) or Related (containing a common undertone hue mixed into all the colors) to the Main character's color.

3. Alliances: Other associates may be depicted in the Main character's color, varied by being used in smaller areas of the costume, or in surface patterns, such as stripes, plaids, checks, prints, or other motifs.

4. Less important but allied characters may use the main color in a print or stripes that are combined with large areas of Neutrals as part of the print. Servants who are major characters in a play, such as Dorine in *Tartuffe*, could fall in this category or in categories 2 or 3 above.

5. Servants' costumes may contain some aspects of an employer's color scheme, as the employer is the Apex character in that relationship. The employer's color may be combined with a Dark Neutral such as Black, Grey, or Brown, plus a Light Neutral such as White, Beige, or Tan. Servants who remain mostly in the background may be in a much Darker and/or Neutralized version of their employer's color, or with very small Accents of the employer's signature color.

6. Characters with more distant relationships to the Main character may repeat a version of the Main character's color in very small costume areas such as

trim, edging, scarves, or neckties, or linings that are seen inside capes, jackets, or other garments.

7. A chorus or crowd may be depicted in a group of similar Neutralized colors, whether or not their colors are the same as that of the Main character.

8. Older characters such as parents of a character may be dressed in Deeper or Greyed versions of that character's color.

9. Younger characters, such as minor children, could wear Pastels, including tints of their parent's color.

10. Weaker relationships to the main character can be portrayed by Neutralized (mixed with the complement of the color) or Subdued (mixed with other colors to lessen the Saturation of the color) versions of the Main character's color.

11. Adjacent colors on the color wheel will suggest a relationship that is more harmonious than the use of complementary colors, which can indicate antagonism between characters.

Structural Function

A character's structural function in the play or the scene helps the mechanics of storytelling and, therefore, can influence color choices. The suggestions below are a starting point for expressing the functions of each character in the script, but each designer will have their own approach. Start with the individual characters:

• Protagonist or Main character: Consider Saturated hues, medium Contrasts, and medium Values for the Main characters, either for areas of their costumes or for entire costumes. The Protagonist usually needs to be clearly seen and to stand out amid the rest of the cast.

• Apex character: This character is at the highest point of wealth, power, and status in the play and is not necessarily the Protagonist. If this character is rich, their colors may be lighter Tints, which can indicate clothing that is not soiled by manual labor, or more Saturated colors, which can indicate wealth because these colors do not appear faded and worn out. Jewel tones, Metallic Gold and Silver, and deep Purple or Red are associated with wealth and power in many societies. Satin, velvet, fur, and jewelry will enhance the look of wealth.

• Antagonist or Obstacle: This character stands in the way of the Protagonist achieving their goal. Therefore, the Antagonist may be dressed in colors that clash with the Protagonist, in opposite colors on the color wheel from those of the Protagonist, in very different categories or Values of colors, or otherwise in a strong contrast to the Protagonist. If the Antagonist reveals their opposition to the Protagonist gradually over the course of the play, their colors may also shift over time.

- Supporting characters, including friends, servants, associates: Depending on their relationships to other characters, whether the Protagonist, Apex, or the Antagonist, these characters may adapt the color schemes of the character(s) to whom they relate, but in less-Saturated form and with less-elegant patterns and textures. The colors may also be used with Neutrals, combined with other colors, and/or used in a surface pattern. This subject is discussed at more length in the Character Relationships section, above.
- Voice of Reason: The Voice of Reason often stands in for the playwright's opinion or expresses the most measured version of social norms. Consider a color that represents reason, truthfulness, and balance – in many societies, Blue may be a good choice.
- Comic Relief: This character may be a counterpoint to the serious action taking place in other scenes, a more amusing version of the Voice of Reason, or a funny sidekick to the Protagonist. The Comic Relief might be in a combination of colors, potentially with some sharp Contrasts, more Saturated hues, and/or mixed Patterns.
- Stock character: *Commedia dell'arte*, traditional folkloric figures, Beijing opera – these characters tend to have a recognizable set of colors, surface patterns, and garments that are known in the culture from which they arise. Take time to research the traditional appearance of these characters, even if you intend to depart from their usual look.

If there is **more than one** Protagonist, Apex character, or Antagonist, decide whether they are evenly balanced in their importance or whether one is more prominent. Further, are they in opposition to one another, allied, or indifferent? In these situations, there are a number of color options. Choose a Complementary color scheme to indicate oppositions, two or more color groups composed of similar Intensities or Values for two or more allied groups, or a color scheme with a clear Dominant color and a Supporting color that harmonizes with the Dominant color, and use the Dominant color more for one group and the Supporting color more for the other group.

Then, move on to the character groupings:

- Chorus/Voice of the community: The Chorus in Ancient Greek theatre moved the action forward and expressed the norms of the community. In modern theatre, the chorus is often a crowd in the background that supports the Protagonist's growth, amplifies the power of the Apex character, expresses societal views, or adds to the spectacle of a musical by singing and dancing. The chorus tends to function as a large unit, often without specific character definition. As such, a closely related set of colors that do not attract attention away from the Protagonist, such as Neutralized Analogous colors, can be a good starting point. In a musical, the chorus may share a group of colors or surface patterns that add visual interest without differentiating individuals apart from their group identity.

• Army: A group of military personnel should be able to be recognized as a group, through the same colors, similar decorations, and the same suite of garments. If this group is associated with the Apex character, they may share some of the Apex character's color or detail. Even if the army is at rest or is not particularly unified in the play, there should be some sort of visual unity despite differences in wear and tear on the garments and differences in how each member of the group wears the uniform.

If there is a **group** of characters that needs to be unified or allied, their colors can help support this sense of unity by use of the same Dominant hue, Tints and Shades of the Dominant hue, prints containing the Dominant hue, Related hues, or Adjacent hues on the color wheel. If it is necessary to show that this character group is separated from other characters, be sure that the other characters have **more** of a difference **between** them and the unified character group than the differences that may exist **within** the unified character group. As long as the differences **within** the group are much smaller than the differences **between** the group and other characters, it will be very clear that the group is reasonably unified within itself but is separate from other characters.

Different Color Approaches to *Romeo and Juliet*

To explore how different designers may design a well-known play with a variety of character types, let's examine how to create the color scheme for a production of *Romeo and Juliet*. Often, the costumes for this play are divided by Temperature, Value, and Hue, with the Montagues in cool, subdued Blues and Greys, and the Capulets in warm Reds and Golds. This use of colors establishes that the two families are strongly opposed to one another. For each family group, there will be unity provided by the colors that are assigned to that group and **not** to the other. At the same time, within each group, there will also be variety, owing to different proportions of the colors that are specifically assigned to that group, along with any base colors of Blacks, Whites, Browns, and/or other Neutrals. Other differences within the group may be expressed with fabric textures, fabric patterns, trimmings, and color placement on the body.

FIGURE 11.1   Montague group in Blues, Greys, and Cool colors

FIGURE 11.2   Capulet group in Reds, Golds, and Warm colors

While there are two large, opposing, unified groups, there are also variations on a theme **within** each group, based on the particular characters' relationships to one another within the group. For example (figure 11.3), Tybalt is a Capulet cousin and is a very hot-headed Antagonist to Romeo, and the Nurse (figure 11.4) is a Capulet servant, an important ally to Juliet, and functions as comic relief. Therefore, Tybalt can be costumed in Saturated colors from the Capulet palette, whereas the Nurse can be costumed in more Neutralized earthy colors that indicate her status as a servant, in addition to accents of Saturated color to show off her comic tendencies and her ties to the Capulet group.

FIGURE 11.3   Tybalt, a Capulet cousin

FIGURE 11.4   The Nurse, an old Capulet servant

For a different production of *Romeo and Juliet*, the costumes for **both** families might be in variations of Gold, Red, and Green, but the costumes will need to have **more unity within each group than between the two groups** in order to avoid confusion. In this example, the costumes for the Montagues may be in shades of Gold, Burgundy, and deep Forest Green and have a greater use of dark Brown and Black, while the costumes for the Capulets may be in brighter hues of Wheat and Yellow Gold, bright Crimson Red, and Yellowed-Green, with a greater use of White and Cream. Therefore, even though the same basic hues are repeated in both groups, the Saturation of the colors and amount of Contrast between the hues would be used very differently in the two families, confirming that they are two **different** groups. However, the contrast between the two groups will be subtler in this version than in the first version of the design. This use of the color scheme would indicate that the war between the families is not as complete as the young soldiers on each side would believe. See figures 11.5–11.7.

FIGURE 11.5   Montagues in lower-value shades of the same color scheme as the Capulets

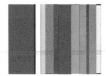

FIGURE 11.6   Capulets in more saturated, warmer versions of the same color scheme as the Montagues

FIGURE 11.7   A selection of *Romeo and Juliet* characters in the same hues, using color Value, Saturation, and level of contrast to differentiate the opposing families

FIGURE 11.8   Color scheme for *Romeo and Juliet*, with the Montagues designed in Blue and Grey and the Capulets designed in Red and Gold. The title characters are dressed in their opposing family color palettes

The lesson here is that, **as long as the differences *within* each group are clearly smaller than the differences *between* the two groups, it will be very clear that the two groups are reasonably unified within themselves but are opposed to each other**. In *Romeo and Juliet*, because the families tend to be physically grouped onstage, a color that is part of the Capulets' palette but is worn onstage by a Montague will appear to be part of the Capulet color scheme and will be potentially confusing to the audience. For example, if the Capulets wear Red and Gold and the Montagues wear Blue and Grey, a Montague character who is dressed in large areas of Gold will seem as if they are in the wrong group.

In the example of *Romeo and Juliet*, we have discussed the opposition of the two families. However, there is also a range of characters **within** the families. There are older and younger characters, those who are reserved and those who are impulsive, and servants and followers, as well as the rich heads of the households. The title Protagonists step away from their families' feud and fall in love. How can color illustrate these character differences?

In consultation with the director's vision, decide whether the family feud – and, thus, the heads of the households and their young followers – is the most important aspect of the play, or whether the relationship of Romeo and Juliet is more important.

If the **family feud** is the most important, the most Saturated versions of the colors within the opposing color schemes can be given to the young people in each family who perpetuate the feud, with Deeper, richer versions of the color scheme and more elegant fabrics given to the older heads of each family, acting as the Apex characters for their own houses. Romeo and Juliet themselves could wear softer versions of their family colors, or an accent of their family's colors along with more Neutral colors, such as Whites, Greys, and Tans, that allow them to share more of each other's family colors in their costumes than the oppositional colors seen on all the other characters. Through colors, these two characters would appear to meet **in between** the opposing groups, but still be part of their original families. See figure 11.8.

If the **relationship** between Romeo and Juliet is most important, it might be appropriate to pick colors for them that are slightly **different** than those worn by their families. For example, if the Montagues wear Blue and Grey, Romeo could wear a Sage Green or a Cool Blue that is similar to colors worn by the rest of his family, but also puts him slightly apart. If the Capulets wear Red and Gold, Juliet could wear a Peachy Rose color that combines Red and Gold but is also slightly different than her family colors, while also coordinating well with Romeo's colors. See figure 11.9.

FIGURE 11.9   *Romeo and Juliet.* The title characters are dressed in colors that are slightly different than – but related to – their family's color palettes

Alternately, Romeo and Juliet may wear accents of **each other's** family colors, so that the characters appear to fit together. See figure 11.10.

FIGURE 11.10   Romeo and Juliet costumed in accents of each other's family colors

Or, both Romeo and Juliet may each wear garments of Green and Rust so that they are in their **own color scheme**, apart from their families' colors. See figure 11.11.

Finally, the production color approach may **evolve** over the course of the play, from a strong sense of the family feud at the start of the play that changes to a focus on the developing relationship between the title characters as the play continues. In that case, **all** of the color approaches outlined above could work at different points in the play, starting with the oppositional colors and moving

FIGURE 11.11   Romeo and Juliet in their own color scheme, apart from their family colors

to color accents from the families set off with Neutrals, towards creating a color scheme that sets Romeo and Juliet closer to one another than to their families. Having said this, this approach will likely end up requiring more total costumes for the production and should be considered carefully by the Costume Designer and Costume Shop manager in terms of budget and labor **before** it is brought to the director!

FIGURE 11.12   Romeo and Juliet in a range of costume colors, moving from their family's color schemes to one of their own

The examples offered above for *Romeo and Juliet* offer several ways of approaching color when planning a production. However, there are many other possible approaches. By being able to analyze the characters' relationships to one another as well as their functions in the play, a costume designer can build a strong foundation of colors to help express the characters and their circumstances to the audience.

Additional Production Examples

Other costume designs further illustrate the use of colors to express allegiances and personalities.

The King Stag – *Color Used to Illustrate Personality and Proximity to Power*

The King Stag by Carlo Gozzi is a play with *commedia dell'arte* characters, set in the fantastical kingdom of Serandip. Deramo, the elegant young King, is in search of a bride. He enlists help for this task from his scheming Prime Minister, Tartaglia, who hopes to install his own daughter, Clariche, as the new Queen. Pantalone, an honest old Counsellor to the king, is father to Leandro (in love with Clariche) and Angela (in love with Deramo and the object of Tartaglia's desires). Brighella, Deramo's foolish butler, coaches his gaudy country cousin, Smeraldina, on how to captivate the King. When Deramo selects Angela as his Queen, Tartaglia uses magic to turn Deramo into a deer during a royal hunting party and to disguise himself as the King. Because of Angela's true love for the King, she sees through Tartaglia's disguise and helps free Deramo from the spell.

FIGURE 11.13   *The King Stag* – Lower register: Pantalone, Leandro, Deramo, Angela, and Tartaglia. Upper register: the Hunter, a peasant, Smeraldina, Brighella, an attendant, and a palace guard

In the production designs shown in Figure 11.13, King Deramo was the Apex character, with the greatest amount of wealth and power, as well as the Main character. His costumes were in satin textures, in light colors to indicate that he did not have to perform manual labor, with a slightly neutralized Red for his vest. The Red vest drew attention to his character and was repeated on other characters around him, including his butler and the palace guards. Angela, Deramo's new Queen, was costumed in Pink (a tint of Red) to show her affinity with Deramo, as well as pale Blue-Green taken from the colors of her father, Pantalone. Pantalone's colors were greyed and slightly faded, indicating his age. Tartaglia, the Antagonist, wore Black, with a darkened shade of Red to indicate his official relationship to the King, and puckered plissé fabric textures to contrast with Deramo's smooth textures. The comic characters, Brighella and Smeraldina, wore a variety of colors and patterns that clashed within their costumes to indicate their lack of restraint or taste. Finally, the Huntsman wore dashes of Red to indicate that he was a minor part of the royal household, and the Peasant was costumed in Browns and in nubby linen textures because he was outside of the royal household.

FIGURE 11.14   *Measure for Measure* government and military characters, with Isabella. Lower register: Escalus, Angelo, Isabella, the Duke. Middle register: Military Police, Officer, Aide to Angelo, Constable Elbow, the Provost. Upper register: the Justice, Soldier, Claudio, Officer, Abhorson as a lawyer

Measure for Measure – *Color Used to Illustrate Two Opposing Social Groups with Their Own Hierarchies*

For the production of *Measure for Measure* shown in Figures 11.14 and 11.15, the government of Vienna was designed as a military state, with the principal authority figures in uniform. The Apex character in this group started as the Duke but was quickly shifted to Angelo when the Duke left Vienna. Within that structure, the characters' differences of status and personality were depicted by the formality of their respective uniforms within a Grey, Black, and White palette and by the number of layers that they wore.

The city of Vienna was designed to contrast with the government that was trying to control the vice around it. In this parallel world, the Bawd was the Apex character and was costumed in a very tight, strapless Red-Orange minidress with

FIGURE 11.15   *Measure for Measure* street characters outside of the military establishment. Lower register: Pompey, the Bawd, Lucio, and Froth. Middle register: a variety of prostitutes, the pregnant Juliet, and the Bawd's Girlfriend. Upper register: Partiers and people on the streets

pinstripes and a Yellow-Orange silk blazer – her "business" uniform. Street characters wore a palette of darkened shades of Saturated colors, with Orange, Yellow, and Fuchsia as the main palette. Garments shapes, surface patterns, and fabric textures were varied, unlike the uniforms of official Vienna, and costumes were body-conscious instead of protective.

Into the Woods – *Color Used to Separate Three Stories that Later Mix Together*

For *Into the Woods*, pictured in Figure 11.16, characters from different fairy tales interacted, all in relationship to the Witch. The Baker, a character who is not from a particular fairy tale, was the Main character who evolves and grows the most throughout the play. The Witch was the Antagonist in most of the stories, as well as being the through-line of the play. The two Princes were of the highest social class, and one had his own attendant to illustrate his power. Jack functioned as comic relief, and Little Red grew up from a child to a young woman during Act 2.

Each fairy-tale group had a different color signature and period silhouette, although the overall design was intended to be more "fairy-tale" than historically accurate. Cinderella's family was in late 1590s Elizabethan costume with a Purple palette, except for Cinderella herself, who was in Blue-Greens. Cinderella was

FIGURE 11.16 *Into the Woods* characters. Lower register: the stepmother, stepsisters Florinda and Lucinda, and Cinderella. Middle register: the Baker's Wife, the Baker, the Witch after her transformation, Jack, and Little Red. Upper register: Rapunzel, Rapunzel's Prince, Cinderella's Prince, Cinderella in her gown as Queen

costumed in a servant's costume from the Italian Renaissance style for her daily clothes and a 1630s style for her gowns – both were more appealing styles than the rest of her family's exaggerated silhouettes. The two Princes, who were notable only for being charming and royal, were costumed in military-inspired tailcoats of the mid-19th century, with capes and riding boots – the fairy-tale vision of a handsome prince. They were brothers and wore the same color palette of Red and Royal Blue, but in alternate positions on their bodies as they are almost interchangeable characters. The Baker and his wife were in a Yellow palette, in a working-class, 18th-century style. Rapunzel was in Pink with an Italian Renaissance silhouette, and Jack and his mother were in rustic Brown and Rust garments from the 1100s. Little Red wore a Red cape (of course) over a late 18th-century folk jacket and dirndl skirt. Finally, the Witch changed from wearing a long black cloak as a story-book witch to a black 18th-century gown with wide court panniers to show off her wealth once she became beautiful at the cost of her magic powers.

Although each character group were costumed in a main color, they also wore garments of each other's colors. In addition, the costumes featured checked trims, geometric patterned fabrics, and plaid surface patterns. These common elements allowed the characters to mix harmoniously with one another during Act 2, when they need to band together to fight the giant who is threatening their homes. They are more of a community than separate households, and their costumes colors helped support this.

The Revolutionists – *A Defined Color Scheme to Create an In-Group and an Outlier*

FIGURE 11.17   *The Revolutionists* – Marie Antoinette, Marianne Angelle, Olympe de Gouges, and Charlotte Corday

In *The Revolutionists*, four women – three real and one a historic composite – discuss liberty and women's rights against the background of the French Revolution. Set inside the mind of feminist writer Olympe de Gouges before her execution, she meets fellow revolutionaries Charlotte Corday, on her way to stab Marat, and Marianne Angelle, a composite character of the enslaved people planning an uprising against the French in Haiti. Marie Antoinette wanders in to complete the foursome, and they debate their hopes, fears, and relationships. In this play, Olympe is the Main character, although Marianne is the most interesting character to watch develop over time. Charlotte inadvertently provides comic relief as well as catharsis, and Marie Antoinette is an Antagonist of sorts, although an oppressive social structure headed by men outside of the stage action is the true Antagonist to these women.

In the production design shown in Figure 11.17, costume research from the mid-1790s period led to a Red, White, and Blue color scheme for the three revolutionaries, as the tricolor scheme was very popular in fashion at the time. Stripes and solid-color garments in cotton or wool were also becoming more fashionable, and these women are costumed primarily in these practical fabrics. Marie, who existed slightly outside of the other women's world, was costumed in a pale version of the color scheme, in Pink, White, and Pale Blue, similar to the colors found on decorative porcelain figurines of the period. Her fabrics were a jacquard brocade with a formal floral pattern, lace, and taffeta with a slight sheen. Marie was from a different social class and political group than the other three women, but she met the same fate as most of them and (in this play) became a friend in the process. Her costume was designed to show that she was a more delicate, less practical character than Olympe, Marianne, and Charlotte, but was also able to blend with the others' colors once they were together on the stage.

12

FLATTERING THE ACTORS

Characters are portrayed by actors. There is a separation between the functions and actions of the **characters** and the human **actors** who inhabit them. Costumes are a tool to bridge this separation and will help an actor present a character, who may be very different than themselves, in a way that an audience can understand and that makes sense within the framework of the play. The separation of character and actor is important for a costume designer to acknowledge and negotiate as they design costumes and interact with actors.

Although we may want to design characters for a play without reference to individual actors, there is a balancing act involved when people put on costumes to become characters in a larger production. Actors appreciate looking their best onstage, and a sensitive costume designer can help them feel confident. A costume is an important tool to help the actor to express the character and transform themselves into a different person in a different time and place.

The **amount** of separation between actors and characters can be interpreted differently by different actors and designers. Actors use their own bodies and personalities to build characters, so they often feel very invested about costume choices and about how they look in their costumes onstage. At the same time, actors need to know that they are separate from their characters, and that the costumes are not what they would wear as ordinary people, but what the **characters will wear for specific situations onstage.** A student actor may feel that they "are" the character and have difficulty distinguishing their own personality and tastes from their approach to acting the character, which makes them evaluate a costume for whether they like it personally rather than whether it is appropriate for the character. It can also be true that a famous actor may bring their own costume suggestions, preferences, or even a personal costume designer to a project. Actors with a relationship with the director and/or with more influence than the costume designer on a project can also affect costume design choices. I have received voicemail messages from actors, listing their preferences for colors and styles of garments for their costumes for a production! (I took their preferences into consideration and evaluated whether those requests would work for the project, then discussed my design rationale for the costumes. This approach made the actor feel respected while also reinforcing the difference between their personal fashion choices and a costume.)

Ideally, costume colors are chosen to support the script, production approach, and character relationships, as the design team works with a director to illuminate a play. The purpose of this chapter is to explore how to consider costume color choices as needed to enhance the actors' appearance and support their work, without disrupting the overall color scheme.

Actor Coloring

Actors' skin tones and hair colors – either natural or with the makeup accents and wigs that will be worn onstage – will be affected by costume color choices. The right costume colors will make the wearer's skin look healthy and set off eye and hair colors. For movies or television, actor coloring and costume colors should be considered together. However, for theatre, the actor is seen at a distance, and an actor's natural coloring may be somewhat altered with makeup and wig or hair colors. Using a slightly Warmer or Cooler version of the correct Value of stage makeup or hair color can improve the color balance between actor and costume. Please note that **I am *not* suggesting that actors wear makeup to appear that they are impersonating a different ethnicity or race than the one with which the actor identifies!** Rather, the opacity of stage makeup and the distance between actor and audience may shift the appearance of Warmth or Coolness in an actor's natural coloring to allow them to successfully wear a color near their face that they would not choose in their own daily life. If the costume color is overwhelming the actor's face, they may need to add a stronger lip color, more blush, or more definite eye shadow or eye liner, to pencil in their eyebrows, or change their hair color with a wig.

Wearing some versions of a hue will make the complexion look smooth and clear, whereas others will dull the appearance of skin, hair, eyes, and teeth. The difference between flattering or unflattering versions of a particular hue could be a matter of color Temperature, Saturation/Intensity, Value, or the level of Contrast with the wearer's coloring.

For example, a character may be designed in a Blue costume, and an actor may look good in Blues, but the Blue that actually flatters the actor is a Warm Blue-Green rather than a Cool Blue-Violet. If adjusting the color Temperature of the actor's makeup and wig colors does not make the costume color look more flattering, consider slightly adjusting the color Temperature of the garment, either through over-dyeing the fabric before building the costume or by adding garment layers or accessories to increase the apparent Warmth or Coolness of an existing costume.

The Saturation and Value of a hue may be as important the choice of hue itself. For example, in the range of variations found on an Orange paint sample card, the colors on one part of the paint card will be much better on a particular actor than other samples on the same card. An individual wearer may look energized in the Saturated Oranges in the center register of the paint card, sickly in high-Value Peachy-Grey tones at one end of the card, and elegant in low-Value Russet tones at the opposite end of the card. Refer to Chapters 3–5 for a more complete discussion of Color Values and Temperatures, with a variety of examples.

Be aware of the amount of Contrast in the actor's coloring between their skin tones, hair color, eyebrows, and eye color. An actor with high-contrast coloring, such as a pale complexion and dark brown hair, brows, and eyes, or a dark complexion with light hair, brows, and eyes, has striking personal coloring that will draw focus onstage. In this case, a medium-contrast combination of colors will be strong enough to hold its own again the actor's coloring without clashing or being overwhelmed by the actor. An actor with low-contrast coloring, such as a dark complexion and dark brown hair, brows, and eyes, has subtle coloring that may be lost onstage without higher-contrast colors being used to call attention to the wearer. Chapter 7 discusses Color Contrasts in more detail.

Flattering costume colors that complement the wearer's coloring create visual continuity between the actor and the costume. On the other hand, if costume colors are unrelated to the wearer's coloring, there may be a strong visual break with their face and hair colors, which in turn will create a strong horizontal line at the shoulders. The result may be that the head looks "lost" if the garment colors are more compelling than the actor's skin and hair colors. At the same time, don't choose colors that are so close to the actor's natural coloring that their face or hair fades into their costume, or that match their skin tone so well that they appear naked from a distance. It is best to choose colors that relate to the actor's coloring, but do not exactly match it.

Practical Solutions

A more-flattering color near the actor's face can be used in order to make a less-than-flattering costume color look better. A necktie or jewelry in colors that relate both to the costume and the actor's hair coloring can create a visual link between the two areas. A flattering scarf or shawl may be draped around the neckline of an unflattering garment so that the garment color never appears adjacent to the wearer's face. On the other hand, if the costume is fading next to the actor's own striking coloring, there are a number of solutions. Add a stronger-hued shirt or blouse, a contrasting t-shirt or camisole under a shirt, a t-shirt or blouse beneath a sweater, a long necklace or necktie that creates a vertical line to link the face to the body, or colored trim to "outline" the ensemble; alternatively, choose more subtle makeup colors to tone down the face area. Earrings, hair accessories, a scarf tied around the neck, or glasses' frames can all help improve the overall color relationship between wearer and costume.

Neutral Garments

Some neutral colors, such as Beige, Taupe, Khaki, Brown, or Tan, can look unflattering against some skin tones. However, expensive garments such as suits and jackets are often in Neutral colors that can be used in a variety of different productions. Neutral colors will tend to be more versatile for future use than a very distinct hue for jackets, suits, trousers, and skirts. If you have a small costume shop, small budget, and/or small costume storage area, the best strategy may be to choose subdued Neutral colors for the expensive garments such as suits and jackets and to use Saturated colors for less-expensive blouses or shirts.

If you find that your best-fitting option for a pulled costume is in Neutral colors that do not flatter the actor's coloring, use hues that flatter their coloring **and** that are also contained within their character's color palette for blouses, shirts, sweaters, or accessories in combination with neutral jackets or suits. The strongest or most Saturated accent colors can be reserved for scarves, neckties, and jewelry.

FIGURE 12.1 Neutrals with Saturated-color "shirt" seen as a small area of color beneath a neutral jacket and lower garment

FIGURE 12.2 Neutrals with Saturated-color "shirt" plus blue accents

Color Placement and Contrasts

Careful placement of colors, Contrasts, Patterns, and Values can affect the apparent shape of actors. Horizontal or busy patterns will draw attention, although the effect will be mitigated if the colors in the surface patterns are closely related.

FIGURE 12.3 Blue variations with patterns. The orientation of the patterns, which are more horizontal than vertical, increase the visual width of the pattern areas

FIGURE 12.4 Blue variations with patterns **and** dark edges. The added dark areas, similar to the open edges of a jacket or cardigan sweater, create more vertical lines. In addition, the greyed tone on the "outer" garment turns the lower horizontal register seen in Figure 12.3 into a more vertical shape

Long vertical edges, or repeats of either the same hue or of closely related Analogous colors, will draw the viewer's eye in a vertical line on the figure, creating a taller appearance.

Placing the patterns on a vertical axis will also create a taller appearance, which will be enhanced by simplifying any patterns. A color repeated at least three times in a costume will create unity even if the area of each repeat is small. If the color repeats occur along an implied vertical axis, it will create a vertical line in the figure.

FIGURE 12.5 Patterns oriented vertically, creating a taller appearance. Simplifying the surface pattern to contain fewer, larger motifs also helps by keeping the viewer's eye from wandering across the composition

FIGURE 12.6 Adding Saturated-color accents and repeating them create an implied vertical line that reinforces the vertical appearance

Bold color contrasts between two Saturated or highly-contrasted hues will call attention to the wearer or to a section of the figure. Bold contrasts tend to **stop the eye at the edges where two colors meet** and can visually subdivide a figure into smaller, usually horizontal, sections because of the lines created at the edges of colors (Figure 12.7).

A Saturated color will add emphasis to wherever it is placed on the body, so place it near the face or on an area of the figure that you want to showcase (Figure 12.8). If horizontal blocks are creating an unflattering effect, adding a long vertical accent in another color will counteract the horizontal lines (Figure 12.9).

A designer may use color to break up the figure either vertically or horizontally if that will be flattering. Strong color contrasts between the top and bottom of a costume can visually cut an actor in half. This can result in the actor looking somewhat shorter and heavier than they really are and draw viewer attention towards the contrasting area and away from the actor's face. For a small actor, do not break up the figure with many horizontal shifts in colors, borders, or contrasts. However, for very tall actors, matching top and bottom garments may be

FIGURE 12.7 High-contrast combination. The Red on the lower area draws more visual focus as the color appears more Saturated than the Green. The point at which the Red and Green meet creates an attention-getting horizontal line

FIGURE 12.8 High-contrast combination with Red on top, drawing visual focus upwards. The smaller block of Red versus Green in this composition, as compared with Figure 12.7, creates a horizontal shape higher up on the body. The **edge** at which the Red and Green meet also creates a high horizontal line. These two high horizontal lines – the Red block and the edge between the Red and Green areas – emphasize the shoulders and draw attention away from fullness in the hips

FIGURE 12.9 High-contrast combination with a vertical center line that draws attention away from the break between the two highly contrasted colors and creates a taller effect

FIGURE 12.10 Complements of Blue and Orange create a strong horizontal visual break where they meet

FIGURE 12.11 Complements of Blue and Orange are slightly Neutralized by some of the complement being added to its opposite hue. A "belt" that is an even more neutralized version of one of these two hues helps avoid a strong visual break between the two areas of color

FIGURE 12.12 Complements of Blue and Orange are neutralized even more than in Figure 12.11, resulting in less contrast and more unity between the two colors. Lengthening the area of the lower color block by raising the waistline position and repeating the skirt color onto the "tights" and "shoes" creates a vertical effect in that area. This will help draw attention away from the hips and towards the face

very overwhelming, and horizontal color accents may be a welcome visual relief because they create smaller horizontal areas within a large vertical space.

If a belt is to be worn at the waist, keep it similar to the colors of the top or bottom garment, or repeat the color of the belt color on the shoes and a necklace to keep the viewer's eye moving in a vertical line up and down the body. Choose closely related colors or textures to flatter a petite figure. For example, match hose color to shoes and then to the skirt for a longer line. See Figures 12.10 – 12.12.

Soft contrasts of hues create a unified appearance. Choosing colors with similar Values of darkness or lightness will be less likely to visually cut the figure into horizontal blocks. Monochromatic tints and shades of a single hue or different hues of the same Value level will help elongate the wearer's figure because the low contrasts won't break the figure into horizontal subsections.

Cool colors tend to draw less attention than Warm colors, so use Cool, Darker, or Subdued colors on larger areas of the figure to reduce focus, and use Warm, Lighter, or Brighter colors on smaller areas to draw focus. For example, in order

FIGURE 12.13 A light color near the face and darker color on the lower part of the body will draw attention upwards. Brighter accent colors and more contrast between colors at the neckline will draw even more focus to the face

FIGURE 12.14 Warm Red-Orange on the upper body with Neutralized Cool Navy on the lower body draws attention to the upper body. A vertical contrasting line reinforces a vertical appearance on the wearer

FIGURE 12.15 Monochromatic tints and shades of Grey create a unified appearance, counteracting the horizontal lines where the tones change. A long vertical accent in a more Saturated color reinforces the vertical effect.

to reduce the apparent size of the hips and increase the apparent size of the chest, color can be helpful. In this case, use a Cool, Dark, or Subdued hue on the bottom half of the figure and a Warm, Light, or Bright hue on the top (Figure 12.13). Use more Saturated accent colors to link the two halves of the figure so that the figure doesn't appear to be cut in half horizontally. Or, use a lighter version of the same color on the top half of the figure, a darker version on the bottom half, and a very dark version on the shoes and/or legs (Figure 12.14). A long thin accent will reinforce the vertical orientation of the figure (Figure 12.15).

Actors will feel supported onstage if they feel that the costume designer is helping them to express their character. If they understand that you are working to make an appropriate overall composition with the costumes, and that you will listen to their worries, they will trust your design choices. Become a partner to the actors, and they will make your costume designs come alive.

13

COSTUME CHANGES

Costume changes will transform the color scheme over the course of a production. Consider how the costume changes advance the audience's understanding of characters and the world of the play before deciding how to use color. Make choices that underline the shifts in action, mood, and character circumstance. Costume changes will add a new level of complexity to a color scheme as colors shift and change over the duration of the play.

For costume changes, it is important to first evaluate **why** the costumes are being changed, as this can lead to somewhat different choices for color usage. No matter the time period of the production, costume changes can indicate a change of season, the passage of a large amount of time, or a special occasion that would require specific garments. The new costumes can be of a different style, color, and/or shape to signal an important shift in the play.

Realistic Modern Dress and 20th-Century Productions

For a realistic modern-day or 20th-century stage production, movie, or television show, costume changes often indicate a new day or a shift in time. In that case, using a similar range of color Saturations and/or Categories (see Chapter 5) for a particular character will maintain a recognizable visual identity. Use a clearly different color or shape of garments from one costume to the next, **within each character's "wardrobe" of hues and garment types**, so that it is clear to the audience that the costume has been changed.

Educating Rita – *Costume Changes to Indicate the Passage of Time and Growth of Character*

In the renderings for *Educating Rita* shown in Figure 13.1, the title character is a 26-year-old working-class British hairdresser who takes an adult education

FIGURE 13.1   *Educating Rita*. The lower register shows the changes for Rita in Act 1; the upper shows her changes for Act 2, along with those for her tutor, Frank

literature class in an attempt to reach outside of her daily life. She states in Act I that she will not buy a new dress until she finishes the class, but the multiple scenes in the act need to be quickly indicated by some type of change in her costuming. For this production, she was designed in a simple denim dress with a variety of jackets, sweaters, and accessories worn over the dress to show the passage of time. For Act 2, Rita is more confident in her growing knowledge and is able to assert herself against her alcoholic tutor, Frank. In this act, Rita was dressed in a greater variety of garment types, with more variety in surface patterns than she worn in Act 1. In contrast, Frank was dressed very similarly throughout the show, except for a change of neckties between scenes and a jacket and trouser change between Acts 1 and 2. The lack of visual changes indicated that his character was not able to move forward with his life at the same time that Rita was expanding her horizons.

Dinner with Friends – *Costume Changes to Indicate an Abrupt Change of Time Period*

FIGURE 13.2   Gabe – Late 1990s and 1980s

FIGURE 13.3   Karen – Late 1990s and 1980s

FIGURE 13.4   Beth – Late 1990s and 1980s

FIGURE 13.5   Tom – 1980s and Late 1990s

In the renderings for *Dinner with Friends* shown in Figures 13.2–13.5, three of the four characters are at a dinner party in the late 1990s at which the fourth character (Tom, Figure 13.5) is discussed because he and Beth (Figure 13.4) are getting divorced. Later, we see the same four characters share a beach house in the late 1980s, on the weekend where Tom and Beth first meet. It was important that the characters were clearly identifiable in this scene, despite period, costume, wig, and glasses changes. Using a consistent palette of colors and types of surface patterns for each character, with alterations in color Saturation, created a visual signature that transcended time shifts.

Private Lives – *Costume Changes to Indicate a Change of Occasion and Mood*

Within the established "wardrobe" of colors and garment styles for each character's range of costumes, costume changes can illustrate a shift in occasion and/or mood. If characters maintain the same outlook and circumstances throughout the play, repeat colors in their costume changes so that they have a color signature, along with variations in color Saturation, Value, use of surface patterns, types of garments, color placement, and different proportions of colors.

In Noel Coward's *Private Lives*, set in 1929, a recently divorced couple discovers that they are unwittingly spending the evening in adjacent hotel rooms in a French resort with their new spouses right after their respective weddings. Sparks fly between the former couple and they run off together to an apartment in Paris, where their jilted partners track them down. Costume changes were important in establishing the mood and social status of the characters and the occasion in each scene, and in indicating the passage of time. The renderings in Figures 13.6–13.9 are from a realized production.

FIGURE 13.6 *Private Lives* – Amanda costume changes

Cream and Taupe were considered very elegant clothing colors in the late 1920s, and Amanda is the most sophisticated woman in the play. In the costume designs shown in Figure 13.6, her evening dress was Cream, rather than the more common 1920s choice of Black, and her dress was in the latest style for 1929, with the waistline almost back at the natural position after the dropped waistlines of the 1920s. In Act 2, she was in a passionate mood, so her pajama colors became less Neutralized and more Saturated than her Act 1 colors. In Act 3, she returned to her signature Cream and Taupe color range with the addition of some Red accents on her suit.

FIGURE 13.7 *Private Lives* – Elyot costume changes

Black and white formal menswear was considered correct evening attire for this time period, and, in Act 1, Elyot was dressed to go out to an elegant evening with his tradition-minded new wife, Sibyl. In Acts 2 and 3, Elyot was matched to Amanda's colors. Despite their constant bickering, Elyot and Amanda were a matched pair in terms of temperament, intellect, and experience, and so their costume colors indicated their similarities.

Briefly married to Elyot, Sibyl is younger, less sophisticated, and holds more conservative values than Amanda, although they exist within the same social class. Sibyl was costumed in floral patterns and in variations of Pink, Mauve, and Blue. Sibyl does not go through a transformation or discernable growth through the play, so her colors and surface patterns remained within a tight range of options, even when her garment types indicated different occasions, such as the evening gown in Act 1 and travelling clothes for Act 3. Sibyl's evening gown was in a floral surface pattern and a

FIGURE 13.8 *Private Lives* – Sibyl costume changes

floaty chiffon material, showing off her youth and femininity. The slightly dropped waistline was starting to go out of style in summer 1929, showing that Sibyl was not as aware the latest fashions as Amanda, despite being the younger character.

FIGURE 13.9 *Private Lives* –Victor costume changes

Briefly married to Amanda, Victor is more conservative and stolid than Elyot. He wore the expected Black and White menswear in Act 1 to go out for the evening. In Act 3, Victor had hastily travelled to the cooler climate of Paris to follow Amanda from the south of France, and so he was costumed in a Grey suit that indicated his conservative nature as compared with Elyot, as well as looking out of place when seen with Amanda's costume.

Period Productions

For a period or Shakespearean production, characters do not necessarily need to change costumes for each day in the script. In some cases, this may be because time is not clearly defined from one day to the next in the script, or because costume changes would slow down the flow of the play as it is staged. Rather, costume changes may be used to indicate different occasions with specific clothing traditions, a shift in the character's evolution during the play, or a definite change of mood. In addition, because period productions can be expensive to costume, and there may be a large number of characters, a costume designer may often save major costume changes for the moments in which the changes will make the most impact.

A Doll's House – *Costume Changes Showing the Development of One Character as Compared with Others*

If characters maintain their outlook and circumstances throughout the play but need to change costumes, choose a limited palette of colors for their costumes so that they have a color signature. Consider reusing characters' signature colors in some manner in their new costumes to maintain the color relationships between characters, using differences in costume shape along with variations in color Saturation, Value, use of surface patterns, types of garments, color placement, and different proportions of colors to show their character transitions.

Written in 1879, *A Doll's House* follows the story of Nora Helmer, a sheltered young wife and mother, through the three days surrounding Christmas when she realizes that her husband considers her to be a lovely possession rather than an intelligent person with hopes of her own.

FIGURE 13.10   *A Doll's House* Costume changes. Lower register – Nora Helmer: Act 1, Act 2, Act 3 party costume and dress in which Nora leaves. Upper register – Torvald Helmer daywear and evening wear, Mrs. Linde, Mr. Krogstad, and Dr. Rank daywear and evening wear

In the production shown in Figure 13.10, Nora started the play in a ruffled Rose-Pink and Russet gown, appearing pretty and impractical. The director was eager to see Nora in warm colors, and so this request was the starting point for Nora's color scheme. In Act 2, Nora was costumed in two darker shades of Red – a variant of Pink – as she realized the peril she was in if her forgery of her father's signature to obtain money to save her husband's life were revealed. In Act 3, Nora was dressed in a folk costume that her husband had chosen for her in which to perform a dance at a party, and so the costume retained some of her character's Reds as well as colors that she may not have chosen for herself. Finally, Nora changed clothing to leave her husband when she realized the emptiness of her marriage. In this case, the script reference about her not actually spending all her allowance on her clothing was a guide, and the Act 1 costume was re-worn, without the ruffled overskirt and lacy cuff ruffles, and with a simpler added inset in the center of the bodice to indicate that her wardrobe was not extensive. Nora returned to her signature colors in the play, but in a simpler and more practical silhouette.

Whereas Nora evolved over the play, the other characters were more constant. Torvald and Dr. Rank, as respectable middle-class men, wore dark Grey and Black frock coats as daywear and Black and White tailcoat ensembles as evening wear. These would have been the expected garment choices for the period. Dr. Rank, secretly in love with Nora, also wore accents of her Red in his neckwear and as a buttonhole flower. Mr. Krogstad was costumed in a Grey-Brown suit with an unmatched vest, showing him as more practical and less wealthy as compared with the other two men in their more elegant daywear. Mrs. Linde, a widow who visited Nora to ask for an office job from Torvald and who inadvertently displaced Krogstad from his job, was costumed in a much plainer dress than Nora would wear. Her dress was made of Brown plaid menswear suiting fabric and in a silhouette that suggested a suit. Mrs. Linde's character was respectable but poor, and so she wore the same costume throughout the production, which also helped to set off Nora's costume changes.

Twelfth Night – *Costume Changes Indicating a Change of Outlook for the Main Characters*

The main characters may be the only characters who change costumes in a production because they are the characters whom the audience is following. Their changes will be more noticeable because they happen against other characters who do not change.

For the production of *Twelfth Night* shown in Figures 13.11–13.13, the characters were costumed in garments from a variety of periods, reflecting their personalities and outlooks on life (also discussed in Chapter 1). Because many of the characters' personalities stayed consistent throughout the play, they were dressed in a single costume throughout the play.

When Viola disguised herself as a man, "Cesario," she retained the color scheme of her original woman's garments. Viola's costume change is an important plot point in the play, in that it fools everyone around her into believing she is a man and identical in appearance to her brother. For this production, her costumes were set in the early 1920s, a period in which women were wearing clothing that was

FIGURE 13.11 *Twelfth Night* costumes. Most characters appeared in a single costume throughout the production, in which characters were depicted in costumes from various periods that expressed their personalities

FIGURE 13.12 *Twelfth Night* – Viola costume changes

more streamlined and masculine, and which also allowed women slightly more social freedoms than earlier periods.

If a character goes through a transition during the play, costume changes that reflect this may cause an adjustment in the production color scheme. The new costume will put that character in a different visual relationship with other characters, which can signal that the character who is changing their costume is the only person who is undergoing growth, while everyone else is static.

FIGURE 13.13   *Twelfth Night* – Olivia costume changes

In this production, Olivia was originally costumed in Victorian mourning. After meeting and being smitten by "Cesario" in her man's 1920s costume, Olivia's new interest was indicated by her changing into a more colorful floral costume of the later 1910s, nearly the same period as Cesario's costume. In her final costume, Olivia was eager to convince Cesario to marry. In this scene, Olivia was costumed in an even more noticeable floral pattern, more Saturated colors, and in a late 1920s style that is even later than the period of Cesario's costume.

The Heiress – *Costume Changes for the Main Character to Indicate a Change in Outlook as Well as the Passage of Time, Small Adjustments for Other Characters*

All the characters in a large production do not necessarily need to change their costumes; often, the costume changes are restricted to the major characters in order to keep the number of costumes and costume budget under control. Depending on the size of the cast and budget, only a few characters might change costumes because they are the characters whom the audience is following. Supporting characters can add accessories or partial costume changes, such as added hats, capes, over-garments, or other pieces in order to suggest a costume change without a full change.

FIGURE 13.14   *The Heiress* – Costume changes for Catherine. Supporting characters had a single costume with a variety of accessories

The costume design for *The Heiress*, shown in Figure 13.14, shows the costume transitions for the main character, whereas many of the supporting characters wore variations on a single costume throughout the play. The character in the lower register is the shy main character, Catherine Sloper, who first appeared in a gown that was remarked upon as being too strongly colored to flatter her. In later costumes, she appeared in a toned-down Blue-Grey color that was more attuned to her personality, and then in elegant lighter colors as she gained confidence through a new romance and a trip to Europe. The characters in the upper register are Catherine's older and less-wealthy widowed aunts. They each wore a single costume, with added accessories, capes, and bonnets to change their appearances for different scenes without making a complete costume change.

Così Fan Tutte – *Costume Changes that Indicate Changing Relationships*

If characters go through a transition in the play, their color stories can change to reflect this. Shifting alliances and developing relationships can inspire a costume change. Costume color can evolve as the characters are affected by one another. For example, if character A is in Red, and character B is in Blue, as character B falls in love with character A, Red can be gradually added to character B's costume or accessories, and Blue can be gradually added to character A's costume and accessories.

The main characters in *Così Fan Tutte* begin as two young, foolish couples; Guglielmo loves Fiordiligi, and Ferrando loves Dorabella. To prove that their sweethearts will be faithful to them, the two men disguise themselves and woo each other's fiancée. The women fall in love with their mysterious suitors, and Ferrando falls in love with Fiordiligi. In the end, the characters marry their original lovers, but all are chastened by their actions.

In the designs pictured in Figures 13.15–13.18, the idea of beautiful-but-foolish **peacocks** was the central metaphor (also discussed in Chapter 5). The couples began the opera by wearing very similar colors, in a range of Blues, with some lighter Pinks and Mauves added to give more variety. The men then wore purposefully inaccurate "exotic" disguise costumes in deeper colors of Blue, Olive, and Purple, with more contrasting hues than their first costumes. As the women start to fall in love, they added over-gowns in colors that coordinated with their new sweethearts' costumes, and they ended the production in long trains that included both the colors of their original and new-found lovers.

Guglielmo began the opera in love with Fiordiligi, and both of them wore a variation of Pink as their main color in this production. His disguise costume was a deep Blue, which was added to Dorabella's later costume changes.

FIGURE 13.15   Guglielmo costume changes

FIGURE 13.16   Fiordiligi costume changes

Fiordiligi began the opera in love with Guglielmo and wore Mauve to coordinate with his Rose Pink coat, but she struggled against falling in love with Ferrando as a disguised suitor. A variation of the Green from Ferrando's disguise costume, Aqua-Green, was added over her Mauve Pink gown as she fell in love with him.

Ferrando began the opera in love with Dorabella and wore a medium Blue coat to co-ordinate with Dorabella's pale Blue gown. His disguise costume was Olive Green.

FIGURE 13.17   Ferrando costume changes.

FIGURE 13.18 Dorabella costume changes

Dorabella started the opera in a Blue gown that coordinated with Ferrando's Blue coat. A variation of the Blue from Guglielmo's disguise costume, Lavender-Blue, was added to her pale Blue gown as she fell in love with him.

Peg o' My Heart – *Costume Changes to Illustrate Social Class*

Peg o' My Heart was a popular play from 1912 in which a wealthy British family, the Chichesters, have just discovered that their bank has failed, leaving them penniless. They begrudgingly agree to take in their poor Irish cousin, Peg, in order to receive money from a bequest. Peg learns to become a lady, proves that she has more common sense than her idle relatives, and wins the heart of the handsome young aristocrat next door. At the end, the Chichesters' wealth is restored, and everyone is happy.

FIGURE 13.19 *Peg o' My Heart* – Peg costume changes

In the early fall of 1912, Peg O'Connor arrives at the Chichesters' mansion in her outdated and shabby travelling clothes. As she was Irish, Green and Blue were designated as her signature colors. She changed into her best dress after she settled in, but it was out of style and too ruffly to be considered elegant, causing consternation in her fashionable relatives. In Act 2, we see Peg a month later in evening clothes. The Chichesters have had ladylike clothing made for her, and her curly hair had been tamed. Peg's evening dress was off-White with pale Pink accents, with a delicate embroidered layer of netting over a Blue-Green silk under-dress. Act 3 took place the next day, after Peg prevented her spoiled cousin Ethyl from eloping with a married man, thereby saving Ethyl from scandal. Peg was dressed in a White cotton eyelet dress, with a Blue sash. Finally, Peg realized that she would never fit in with the Chichesters and changed back into her original travelling clothes in order to leave.

FIGURE 13.20 *Peg o' My Heart* – Mrs. Chichester costume changes

Mrs. Chichester is the conservative matriarch of the family who disdains Peg for being Irish and who dotes on her own spoiled children. When faced with the prospect of being poor, she agreed to take Peg in and to train her to be a lady. She was exasperated by Peg and was an Antagonist to her. Mrs. Chichester's costume colors were in the same value range as her children's costumes, with more greyed tones to help indicate her age. In Act I, she wore a Blue-Grey and Taupe suit with White accents. In Act 2, she was dressed in dull Lavender and Black for evening. When she was awakened by the noise of Ethyl arguing with Peg about an elopement with Mr. Brent, her Cream robe and cap were trimmed in Greyed Lavender. Finally, as Peg was leaving the house, Mrs. Chichester was dressed in a Grey and Lavender plaid overdress with a pale Grey under-dress.

FIGURE 13.21 *Peg o' My Heart* – Ethyl costume changes

Ethyl Chichester is the spoiled daughter. She is idle and horrified that the family is now poor and may have to work for a living. She flirts with Mr. Brent, a married man who convinces her to run off with him. In Act 1, Ethyl was designed in a pale suit with a narrow skirt in tones of Cream and Taupe, for a refined appearance that contrasted with Peg's garments and unkempt hair. In Act 2, Ethyl was costumed in evening clothes, consisting of a Golden Bronze lace overdress with Green-Blue under-dress and burnt Orange accents, as she decides to run off with Mr. Brent. Finally, the morning after Peg had disrupted her plans, Ethyl wore a Golden Yellow jacket and a pale Cream with celery Green pinstriped skirt with a Blue belt; her signature pale colors were slightly more saturated, and she took on some of Peg's colors after Peg saved her reputation.

Alaric Chichester is the idle rich son, until his family is no longer rich. He was dubious of his mother's plan to turn Peg into a lady and even more dubious of

FIGURE 13.22 *Peg o' My Heart* – Alaric costume changes

his mother's instructions that he propose to Peg in order to get her inheritance. In Act 1, Alaric was dressed for an afternoon of strolling the grounds in a Cream jacket, slacks, tennis sweater, and a boater hat. His accents were Blue, creating a color range that was similar to Jerry's but with less depth. In Act 2 he was in evening wear – a tuxedo with a Black vest (an option for the time period) to wear for a dinner at home. He was later seen in a robe and pajamas when awakened by Peg's argument with Ethyl. In Act 3, he ended the play much as he began it, in an unmatched costume of Creams with Blue accents. In order to show his wealth, Alaric changed costumes, but the costumes themselves did not display a large range of differences except for indicating the time of day and occasion of the scenes.

FIGURE 13.23 *Peg o' My Heart* – Jerry costume changes

Jerry is the handsome neighbor, who is actually Sir Gerald Markham. He befriends Peg, and she falls in love with him. He was charmed by her and proposed to her at the end, despite her being in her own, unfashionable clothing. Jerry's clothing was designed to be in style and elegant but not ostentatious, as Peg is unaware of his aristocratic status. His signature colors were Blue-Grey, Cream, and Taupe. He was the romantic partner to Peg, and their colors grew similar as she became a lady and he began to love her.

Mr. Brent is a bored married man who flirts with Ethyl and tempts her to elope with him. He is a country landowner and was costumed in a Brown tweed Norfolk jacket to reflect this. However, as he was rich, his garments fit perfectly for a look that was elegant and not rustic. His Act I Rust vest was echoed in the burnt Orange accents on Ethyl's Act 2 costume. In Act 2, Brent added a long Tan motoring coat, silk driving scarf, driving cap, and goggles for the intended elopement.

FIGURE 13.24   *Peg o' My Heart* – Brent costume changes

The Taming of the Shrew – *Costume Changes to Create Disguises, Show Character Progression, and Illustrate Different Occasions*

The Taming of the Shrew is a problematic play to put on in modern times and is often softened to be more palatable for a modern audience who is not likely to accept Petruchio's methods of controlling a woman. Petruchio is on the hunt for a rich wife in Padua and agrees to woo the brash Katerina in order that the young men in town might be free to woo her younger, sweeter sister, Bianca. In the modern-dress production pictured in Figures 13.25–13.29, the problematic aspects of Katerina's "taming" were not softened.

FIGURE 13.25   *The Taming of the Shrew* – Petruchio costume changes

Petruchio was pictured as a "man's man," with a slight stubble beard and an attitude. His color range was Taupe, Grey, Burgundy, and Rust. He arrived in Padua in a fur trimmed jacket and a leather vest and then changed into a Burgundy shirt, jacket, and a long loose coat for his meeting with Katerina. After having struck a bargain with her father for an ample dowry, the play indicates that his appearance at their wedding was intended to humiliate his bride; in this production, he appeared on a rolling wagon, wearing mismatched garments that were oversized and ridiculous, in clashing colors and patterns. At his country house, Petruchio wore grimy Tan overalls and his leather vest while he broke Katarina's spirit. Finally, wearing a business suit and tie, he and Katerina returned to Padua

FIGURE 13.26   *The Taming of the Shrew* – Katerina costume changes

for Bianca's wedding to Lucentio, where Petruchio was to receive his reward for making Katerina more docile.

Katerina, who is written as an Antagonist to Petruchio, has a mind of her own that conflicted with social norms of female behavior. Because she was the oldest sister, she needed to be married before her more conventionally desirable younger sister could be wooed. She was costumed in dark colors to contrast with Bianca's brighter pastels, and in pants and a leather jacket to give her a sturdier appearance than Bianca's short dresses. Prior to her wedding, she did not change costumes, contrasting with Bianca's numerous costume changes. For her wedding, Katerina was dressed in a puff-sleeved wedding gown that she would never have chosen for herself, making her look like a sweet princess when she was in fact very angry. When she was at Petruchio's estate, she was dressed in a dull Olive bathrobe, Burgundy plaid shirt, boxer shorts, and thermal pants, all cast-off items from Petruchio, in order to keep her away from her familiar clothing choices. Finally, at Bianca's wedding, she was dressed in a conservative Burgundy coat dress, as the vision of the perfect wife. Katerina's costumes were largely made up of garments that she would **not** have chosen for herself, in order to show that she was being forced to give up her personality to achieve the transformation that all the other characters desired of her.

FIGURE 13.27   *The Taming of the Shrew* – Bianca costume changes

Bianca was presented as the perfect daughter: sweet, docile, beautiful, and desirable. She was a daddy's girl with an extensive wardrobe. Bianca was designed in a range of bright pastel colors, short skirts, and fashionable looks that would be appealing to her many suitors. She was a bridesmaid at Katerina's wedding, in a puffed-sleeve floral dress that had a silhouette similar to Katerina's wedding gown. For Bianca's own wedding to Lucentio, she wore a figure-hugging, one-shoulder lace gown with a net train and a floor-sweeping bridal veil.

Lucentio is a young man smitten with Bianca, who turns to Petruchio to remove the impediment of the unmarried Katerina and who turns to his

FIGURE 13.28   *The Taming of the Shrew* – Lucentio costume changes

friends to help him woo Bianca. His color signature was Tan, Rust, and Green – warm and friendly colors. He began the play in a sweater and corduroys, then exchanged clothing with his servant, Tranio, in order to speak with Bianca unnoticed by her family. Later, he was disguised in a tweed jacket with elbow patches and corduroy pants with bike clips at the hem to present himself as Cambio, a tutor, in order to spend time alone with her. He attended Katerina and Petruchio's wedding in a Black and White tuxedo. For his own wedding to Bianca, Lucentio and his male attendants wore pale Grey tails, as his bride would want something even more special to be worn by the attendants than was worn at her sister's wedding.

FIGURE 13.29   *The Taming of the Shrew* – Hortensio costume changes

Hortensio was designed to be a college buddy of Lucentio, helping him find a way to woo Bianca. He wore dull Orange and Olive as his signature colors, relating him to Lucentio. Later, he disguised himself with a Purple jacket, an ascot, and a goatee as the (jazz) Music Master.

Shakespeare's plays use a variety of minor characters and servants to amplify the power of the major characters and to provide subplots. Part of the fun of designing these characters is the opportunity to make a bold statement that will be seen onstage for a short time. In addition, numerous minor characters are often played by a limited number of actors, so strong color and garment silhouette differences between each actor's many characters can help disguise the actors and add more interest to the production color scheme.

Costume changes that are indicated by the script, whether by a time change, by character growth or change of circumstances, or by different occasions in the play, can add a new level of complexity to creating a color scheme. As colors shift

FIGURE 13.30 *The Taming of the Shrew* — Servants and Minor characters. Lower register: Vincentio, the Haberdasher, the Tailor (a tribute to many fabulous costume designers I have met), and the Pedant (with a pocket protector). Upper register: Servant at Katerina and Petruchio's wedding, four of Petruchio's foolish servants on his country estate, and Grumio

and change over the course of a production, use the costume changes to advance the audience's understanding of the characters and the world of the play. Maintain a palette of colors for each character so that they have a color signature and use changes in the palette to indicate when the character has made an important internal change or when the mood of the production has changed.

14

DISTRIBUTING COLOR

Having explored ways to derive a color scheme and theories about how to use colors in combination, we get to what may be the most difficult part of using colors – making the decisions about which colors will be used for which costumes. Some designers avoid the moment of decision as long as they can put it off, pushing back other decisions in the process. This may also affect the costume shop schedule and push back the rest of the decision-making time line.

Even with decades of experience, making color decisions is something that I tend to put off by endlessly searching for more fabric swatches and trying multiple rounds of dye tests in order to delay the final decisions, with the hope that I will find the perfect colors that will magically pull the show together. I can report, however, that the magic moment doesn't tend to arrive, and it is necessary to just sit down and make some definite choices in order to move on with the design.

Color is a very important element in designing stage costumes. The audience may not fully understand the nuances of period details, but they will be attuned to how color is used for various characters. Because color can be so impactful, it may become a source of stress for a designer. To assist in making decisions, this chapter will take you through an approach to distributing color within a group of costumes. This method will work both for obvious "Color Schemes" to create a stylized effect, or to create a less-obvious sense of color unity that does not appear "designed" but that looks harmonious.

The discussion in this chapter assumes that the designer is creating color renderings of the production. However, even if formal costume renderings will not be presented to anyone else, it is useful to plot out color options and configurations before making decisions. The illustrations in this chapter are a combination of separate drawings from different productions, grouped together on a single page for use in quick color explorations.

At the point in the design process where is it necessary to make definite color decisions, take a look back at any garments that you have pulled or purchased and at fabrics that you plan to use for the show. Assemble small color swatches in a group to preview the overall color effect, or assemble all the garments that have been chosen to be used for potential costumes on a wardrobe rack or a group of dress forms, and take photographs for reference. Remember to measure the garments to avoid falling in love with garments that have no chance of being worn by a particular actor. Once you have a sense of the garments that will fit the actors playing various characters, work from what you have. If costumes will be built for the main characters, determine which colors will work with the pulled items and shop for appropriate fabric in those colors. Most importantly, try to review all the available options before starting renderings in order to lessen the volume of decisions to be made while trying to add color to the costume designs.

If you are creating renderings, I strongly suggest **making copies of the drawings before you start painting them**. I use colored makers on 17" by 11" 90wt. copy cardstock for my own renderings, partly because I can copy my drawings onto the paper using a copy machine and can make multiple copies if I want to experiment with different color options. (I have also been known to glue areas of recolored paper onto renderings where I have revised the color on one garment and did not want to redo the entire rendering. Renderings are a **tool**, not the end point of design.) If you prefer to work with watercolors, consider making black and white copies of your drawings and testing out colors with color pencil or quick swathes of watercolor before sitting down to carefully paint the renderings. Other designers prefer to scan their drawings and use a computer to fill in colors so that they can see different options. In any case, it takes a great weight off the color decisions and allows for a freer attitude towards trying options if a designer is not worrying about ruining precious drawings that would take hours to reproduce.

Different options for several costumes in a production are shown in Figures 14.1–14.10, with colors quickly added in felt pen to see what the colors would look like before committing to a specific costume design:

The four costumes in Figures 14.1–14.4 and the six in Figures 14.5–14.10 were developed for a production in which the set design became increasingly bright as the scene designer tested paint samples. In response, the costume color tests became bolder each time a new color combination was considered. Using these quick color studies, I was able to "sneak up" on a bolder color scheme than I had originally planned and to make better decisions **before** fabric needed to be purchased.

FIGURE 14.1   Dark Green coat

FIGURE 14.2   Orange coat

FIGURE 14.3   Purple striped coat

Process for Distributing Colors

When it comes to the point of organizing a group of colors into a set of costume drawings, the goal is to **distribute the colors in order to enhance the relationships in the script and the mood of the specific production**. Here is a practical approach to get over the stress and to get the process started.

FIGURE 14.4   Final color choice for the production

FIGURE 14.5   Purple changeable gown

FIGURE 14.6   Teal gown

Start with the Knowns

Quite simply, it is helpful to break the task down into segments and to **work on what you know until it is time to make major decisions**. Usually, there are aspects of the color scheme that can be filled in with known hues before the more difficult color decisions have to be made.

FIGURE 14.7   Final costume choice for the production

FIGURE 14.8   Soft Rust gown

FIGURE 14.9   Yellow gown with Red stripes

FIGURE 14.10   Final costume choice for the production

1. Begin by **filling in the skin tones and hair colors** of the actors, whether natural to the actor or altered with wigs. If the show has not yet been cast, leave these areas blank until you have information with which to fill in these areas. If there are characters where wig or hair colors are not yet chosen, wait to fill in these areas until after making more of the costume color decisions, as the hair colors can be used to balance out the garment colors, but move on to the next step. If this is a paper project, fill in skin and hair coloring as you wish, not forgetting that, **in a modern production, the actors will be cast from a variety of heights, weights, ethnicities, and races**. Be mindful of this in order to create a portfolio that contains a range of sizes, shapes, and ethnicities.
2. Choose the Light and Dark Neutrals for the costumes that will be repeated throughout the scheme, which are usually found in shirts, hosiery, headgear, and footwear. Some designers refer to the Light and Dark Neutrals that unify costumes in a larger production as the "Show White" and the "Show Dark," or as "Utility" colors.

   Light neutrals such as White, Off-White, Cream, Tan, Pale Taupe, and Pearl Grey often are used for shirts, undergarments, and hosiery. Dark Neutrals such as Black, Dark Brown, or Charcoal are often used for shoes, skirts, trousers, and hats. Often, this boils down to White-range shirts and Black shoes for many period productions, or Beige-tone shirts and Brown-tone shoes for more rustic productions.

FIGURE 14.11 Neutral colors filled in as a starting point for adding other colors

3. Next, **fill in the colors you know will be in the production**. In other words, there may be known blocks of colors based on the types of costumes in the show. For example, if the play has a scene with several men in formal-wear, the men will create a large block of Black tuxedos or tails with White accents. When rendering, be sure to actually use a solid **real** Black, rather than a faded Grey, to indicate the Black costumes. This dark color is accurate to what will be seen on stage, and will free you to incorporate stronger colors in the costumes yet to be colored.

   A play with characters in uniform will have a large block of the uniform colors as part of the color scheme. A play with religious or clerical garb will have a large block of those colors. If many men are in suits, dark and subdued Blacks, Greys, and Blues will tend to dominate the scene. If outerwear is part of a scene, dark colors are likely to make up a large part of the costumes. In all cases, when filling in the renderings, **give a sense of the real depth of the colors and the quantity of those colors** as related to any other colors. If you like to use soft colored pencils or wispy watercolors, push yourself to depict the actual color tone and weight that will be on stage – no pale Greys or light Blues representing what will actually be solid Black or deep Navy! When there is a clear depiction of the actual depth and amount of color that will be on stage, a designer can make better choices with the garments for which color choices still need to be made.

Once all of these colors are added to the renderings, the renderings are likely to be nearly half completed, and the number of color decisions will have been reduced to a more manageable number. The once-blank pages are no longer so empty, and the choices left to be made are less overwhelming.

Assess the Character Relationships

Color can help illustrate the relationships on stage and can be a very useful way to help the audience keep track of characters. Refer to Chapter 11 for a much fuller discussion of using color to define characters.

Group the costume drawings that need to refer to one another next to each other on your work surface. It is very helpful to **actually place the drawings for related characters together before starting to add color to the renderings**. If multiple drawings are on a single sheet of paper for the final renderings, I suggest making small thumbnails of the drawings so that they can be moved and colors can be tested **before** they are added to the renderings.

Here are the steps to follow:

1. **Decide on the Main character and radiate outwards**. If there is a Main character with whom every other character has a relationship, establish the main color for the central character and then repeat the color in different

FIGURE 14.12   Menswear colors added

amounts, placements, fabric textures, surface patterns, and color intensities for the other characters, based on their relationship with the central character. The Main character is usually the Protagonist, but there may be exceptions to this situation. (From this point, the terms Main character, Central character, or Protagonist will be used interchangeably.)

In terms of building a color scheme, the **Main character is the one who has clear relationships with the majority of the rest of the characters onstage**. The centrality of the Main character should be clear to the audience from the color choices, unless the Main character needs to be inconspicuous for a particular reason.

2. **Assess who must relate to this character.** Other characters may be part of the Main character's Family, with older and younger members, the Main character's Lover/Romantic Interest, Business Associates, Friends, Allies, Servants, Antagonists, or Chorus/Crowd/Background Characters. Chapter 11 discusses in detail how to use color to illustrate characters and their relationships.

Tell the Story of the Play, the Characters, and Their Relationships through Color

Choose a signature or Dominant color for the Central character. Once the Dominant color is chosen, it can be adapted to illustrate various characters with

different Values and levels of Saturation. The Size of the area that the Main character's Dominant color covers can be varied for use in other characters' costumes,
based on their relationships to the Main character. For example, if the Main character is costumed in a full-length garment of a particular color, such as a Blue
gown or suit, closely related characters may repeat the same Blue in a smaller
segment on the figure, such as a jacket, vest, blouse, or shirt.

Fill in areas of the renderings with the Main character's color, in the sizes and
Intensities that are reflective of the different characters' relationships with the
Main character. Tints (added White), Shades (added Black), Tones (added Grey),
Neutralized (added Complement), or Subdued (added color to adjust the base
hue in a particular direction) variations of the Dominant color will illustrate a
weaker relationship to the Main character than full-strength repeats of the main
color would indicate.

In the example discussed above, the Main character's signature color becomes
the Dominant color of the overall color scheme, varied to indicate character
relationships. However, the central character's color does not have to extend
throughout the rest of the costumes if you do not intend to create a noticeable
color scheme. In that case, choose **similarities** in color such as Analogous or
Related colors, or similar levels of color Intensity, Value, and/or use of surface
pattern between the central character and their allied characters. For example, if
the Main character wears Green as a signature color, their allies may be put in
Blue-Greens, Blues, and/or high-Value/low-Intensity Yellow-Greens to indicate
their relationships.

Examples of how the central character's color may be diffused to other characters are discussed in Chapter 11 and below. You may find it helpful to start filling
in the Main color of the color scheme in the order of relationship to the central
character, which is reflected in the ordering below.

1. Love interests or partners may repeat the Main character's color.
2. Friends and partners may be in a version of the Main character's color, in
   smaller amounts of that color, or in **similar** colors, such as Analogous hues
   to the main color, Related colors, or hues with the same color Temperature,
   Intensity, and Value as the main color.
3. Other associates may be depicted in the central character's color, varied by
   being used in smaller sizes or in surface patterns.
4. Less-important allied characters may use the main color in a surface Pattern or
   stripes that are diluted with plenty of Neutrals to indicate a weaker relationship.
5. Servants' costumes may contain some aspects of an employer's color scheme.
6. Other characters may repeat a version of the Main character's color in small
   areas such as accessories.
7. Pastels may be used for children.
8. Shades or Grey-toned versions of colors may be used for older characters.
   For example, older characters can be put in dark Green, Navy, and shades of

Neutralized Purples in a situation where the Main character wears medium-value Green, Blue, and Purple.

9. Saturated versions of a color may be used along with light Neutrals for wealthy characters, as these hues appear as if the costume is newer and the character does not have to perform physical labor.

10. Lower-intensity (whether Neutralized with its complement, mixed with Black to create a Shade, Toned-down by being mixed with Grey, or Subdued by being mixed with Brown or other hues to lessen the intensity) versions of the main color may be used for less-wealthy characters or laborers, as these colors appear as if the costume is older, has been washed repeatedly, and/or is stained through physical labor.

If you are simply not able to make a color choice, it is helpful to choose one "If in doubt, make it [choose a color]" **default** color such as Blue, Yellow, Red, Black, Brown, Grey, Beige, and so on. The default color will end up being a large percentage of the color scheme. Any time you cannot make a color choice, use the default color, and a de facto color scheme will emerge. Having a default color ends up being a good way to unify any garments that haven't yet been assigned a color. Different default colors may be used each for shirts, hosiery, footwear, or other garments.

FIGURE 14.13 One hue is distributed around the costumes, with variations in Intensity and large areas of White

If you simply cannot make a color decision, Blue is a safe default color choice because it is seen mostly positively in most cultures around the world, although even Blue has some negative associations for particular audiences. See Appendix 1 for color meanings in different cultures around the world.

Fill in all of the areas that you can with the Dominant color. You will come back to this color as you incorporate additional hues into the color scheme.

Pick a Second, Supporting Color that Coordinates with the Dominant Color

The Supporting color can be a hue that blends attractively with the Dominant color, such as a brick Red Supporting color to a tile Blue Dominant color. Or, the Supporting color may be opposite from the Dominant color on the color wheel to create a dynamic scheme or to portray a rivalry. For a two-color scheme, large areas of the colors are easier to coordinate if one or both colors are **not** Saturated hues. For example, tile Blue and brick Red tend to appear more harmonious together than fully Saturated bright Blue and bright Red. See Chapters 4 and 5 for a fuller discussion of how to coordinate multiple hues in a color scheme.

Add the Supporting color to the renderings, using this color to reinforce character relationships:

- Characters who are not particularly related to the central character may use more of the Supporting colors, either with small areas of the Dominant color or with more of the show Neutrals.
- If the Dominant color is fully Saturated, the Supporting color may be less-Saturated or a Tint, Shade, Tone, Neutralized, or Subdued color rather than a Saturated hue. For example, with a Dominant bright Red, consider dull Teal, Greyed-Green, soft Butter Yellow, or deep Grey as a Supporting color.
- If the Dominant color is **not** at full Saturation, the Supporting color may be more Saturated or fully Saturated. For example, with a dominant Blue shade that has some Black mixed with it, consider a sharp Burnt Orange, intense Purple, or Grass Green as a Supporting color.
- **Two Saturated and contrasting** Dominant and Supporting colors may be used if there are plenty of Neutrals in the scheme to act as buffers between the contrasting colors. This will create a lively color scheme that may be appropriate for a comedy or musical.
- Two less-Saturated Dominant and Supporting colors may be used together if there will be strong Accent colors to enliven the scheme in at least a few areas. This will create a more understated color scheme than one featuring full-Intensity colors in the Dominant and/or Supporting positions, because the full-Saturation accent colors in this case will be in smaller areas relative to the less-Intense Dominant and Supporting color areas.

FIGURE 14.14 Supporting Color added

Choose the Accent Color(s)

A third, more-saturated Accent color will add interest to the color scheme and allow the designer to make many more color combinations. Accent colors are often used in small areas and, therefore, may be of higher Intensity/Saturation than the Dominant and Supporting colors. Neckties, scarves, pocket squares, linings, socks, hair decorations, jewelry, suspenders, sashes, belts, vests, shoe accents, and accessories are good places to use Accent colors.

- Accent colors may be repeated in greater or lesser amounts in various costumes throughout the color scheme.
- Accent colors may be used around the actors' faces to draw audience focus.
- Different Accent colors may be assigned to each character to create more naturalistic effects and to show off character individuality through the color scheme.
- Strong Accent colors may be used for garments where one would expect a light Neutral, such as shirts or hosiery, or a dark Neutral, such as shoes and hats, to enliven and unify a color scheme with costumes gathered from different sources. As a color scheme develops in real life, it sometimes becomes clear that using more Saturated colors instead of Neutrals on the shirts, hosiery, footwear, and headdresses will better serve the overall balance of the color scheme. In that case, tinting hosiery to an Accent color and/or

adding Accent-colored edging trim to garments can help enliven the color combinations.

In addition, adding a third color to the Dominant and Supporting colors will **extend the overall color scheme** and will allow the designer to "triangulate" the colors, using different proportions of the Dominant, Supporting, and Accent colors on different costumes in order to distribute the colors with interesting variations. Different possible combinations include:

- **For approximately 60% of the costumes, or costumes that are on the stage the most:**
  - All color A
  - Color A plus Neutrals
  - Color A in various Tints and Shades
  - Color A plus Black and White
  - Color A plus color B in ⅝ vs. ⅜ proportions
  - Color A plus color B plus Neutrals
  - Colors A and B in a print
  - Color A plus color B in various Tints and Shades
- **For approximately 30% of the costumes, or costumes that are on stage less, or groups that are not as centered around the Main character:**
  - All color B
  - Color B plus Neutrals
  - Color B in various Tints and Shades
  - Color B plus Black and White
  - Color B plus color A in ⅝ vs. ⅜ proportions
  - Color B plus color A plus Neutrals
  - Color B plus color A in a print
  - Color B plus Neutrals and small accents of color A
  - Color B plus color C in various Tints and Shades
  - Color B plus color C in ⅝ vs. ⅜ proportions
  - Colors B and C in a print
- **For approximately 10% of the costumes or costumes that are seen briefly, are for special moments, or create accents onstage:**
  - All color C
  - Color C plus Neutrals
  - Color C in various Tints and Shades
  - Color C plus Black and White
  - Color C plus color A in ⅝ vs. ⅜ proportions
  - Color C plus color A plus Neutrals
  - Colors C and A in a Print

- Color C plus Color A in various tints and shades
- Color A in tints and shades plus 10% accents of Color B
- Color A in tints and shades plus 10% accents of Color C
- Color B in tints and shades plus 10% accents of Color A
- Color B in tints and shades plus 10% accents of Color C
- Color C in tints and shades plus 10% accents of Color A
- Color C in tints and shades plus 10% accents of Color B.

(There are more possible combinations, but this list is a good starting point.)

This distribution above allows for many different combinations of colors in a three-color scheme, with differences of Proportion, Tints, Shades, and Tones of each hue, as well as Neutrals. Although all of these combinations may not be appropriate for a particular show, they can help give options for adding colors while you are trying to pull a production together with a limited color scheme.

If you have distributed the colors to your renderings and the colors still lack visual cohesion, adding wide trim or lace edging to each costume can add unity. See Figures 14.15 and 14.16.

FIGURE 14.15 Garments without trim

FIGURE 14.16 Garments with unifying trim

A Decision Tree for Choosing Colors in Two Scenarios

The discussion in this chapter may be too much to wade through when all you really want are some quick directions on how to proceed with choosing colors. Here are two scenarios from which to start that summarize the discussions elsewhere in this book and this chapter. There are many other possible scenarios that fall somewhere in between the two presented here; feel free to mix and match in order to find a method that works best for your circumstances.

Scenario I

A production with plenty of resources to allow for maximum choice in design, or a "paper" (hypothetical or class) project. If the show is being rendered, fill in the appropriate colors after each step below.

1. Determine the character relationships within the script. Start from the central character and work outwards to include love interests, partners, friends, servants, allies, and opponents. If rendering the production, arrange the uncolored costume renderings on your work surface to show off the character relationships in terms of proximity to the Main character.
2. Choose the Light and Dark Show Neutrals for the color scheme.
   Or
   Consider the skin and hair tones of the actors. The actors' coloring may be an important aspect of the overall color impression that will be created. If the show has not been cast at the start of this process, color Temperatures (Chapter 6) or Contrasts (Chapter 7) may be adjusted as the design process continues. If this is a paper project, vary the characters' sizes, shapes, coloring, and other characteristics to embrace potential actors' differences.
3. Choose a signature costume color for the Main character. Often, this Dominant color will be of a medium Intensity and Value in order to allow for variations of the color to be used for related characters.
4. Repeat the Main character's color as the Dominant color throughout the web of other characters, including variations of Value, Intensity, Placement, and use of the colors to illustrate relationships:
   a. Love interests may repeat the Dominant color.
   b. Friends and partners may be in a somewhat darker or lighter version of the Dominant color.
   c. Less-important but allied characters may use the Dominant color in a subdued version, as a Similar color, and/or in a print.
5. Choose the Supporting color for the color scheme. Use this color (which may be more than one hue if the production has many costumes or several competing factions) to set off the Dominant color, to establish a secondary web of influences with a group of characters, and/or to add visual interest.

6. Choose Accent colors for the characters. Accent colors are often used in small areas and, therefore, can be of higher Intensity than the Dominant and Subordinate colors. Accent colors may be used around the actors' faces to draw audience focus, and Accent colors may be different for each character. For a more unexpected effect, use accent colors in places where one would expect a Neutral.
7. Repeat the Dominant, Supporting, and Accent colors around the costumes to create unity and to illustrate any relationships. Evaluate the overall balance in the renderings and assess whether the renderings reflect the relationships correctly.
8. Fill in any blank costume areas with a default color, or with a variety of colors that harmonize with what is already on the renderings.

Scenario II

A modern-dress production, or for costumes in a situation without resources to construct an entire production.

1. Pull costumes from any available stock and/or purchase items that may be returned for a full refund.
2. Try costumes on actors for fit and appropriateness. Take photos to record the colors and fit of the garments that will potentially be used.
3. If available, put garments on dress forms to see the group as a whole. If no dress forms are available, hang garments as ensembles on hangers on a rack, or arrange the fitting photos to show character relationships.
4. Determine if the **colors of the garments available** will form the basis of a color scheme that works for the production. With the colors that exist, **start with the Main character** and work outwards to indicate the relationships between that character and their partners, friends, servants, and opponents. See further discussion of this in Scenario I, above.
    a. If possible, the most interesting colors should be used for Main characters and may be repeated in secondary characters/servants/love interests to show associations of characters.
        And/or
    b. The Main character may be costumed in a clearly different color than everyone else to draw focus through variety (e.g., Hamlet in Black while the rest of the court is in higher-Saturation/more festive colors; Romeo and Juliet in colors that set them apart from their family groups).
        And/or
    c. The costumes as a whole may be in a similar **category** of color (Warm colors/Cool colors/ Bright colors/Pastels/Neutrals, etc.) to create the overall visual world that supports the script. Specific accessories, trim, or details may then be added to emphasize the Main character and their relationship to the other characters.

5. Add strategic colors to reinforce the developing color scheme. Use shoes, socks, shirts, belts, accessories, costume layers, hair accessories, hats, scarves, and neckties to pull the costume colors together. Accent colors used in places where one would expect a light neutral such as for shirts or hosiery, or a dark neutral such as for trousers and shoes, will add even more interest to a color scheme.

No matter which colors you choose, color distribution should be carefully thought out in order to create overall unity. Make sure one hue or closely related group of hues dominates the composition in terms of size, that there are contrasts in the Values and in the relative Saturation of the hues, and that the hues repeat within the composition. Contrast the Dominant hue with a Supporting hue and one or more Accent colors. Prints and surface patterns can be used to extend the color scheme and to add visual interest.

Distributing Colors in Costume Renderings in Three Examples

The following renderings show the process of distributing colors in three different groups of costumes. There are points where several different combinations are considered, or where changing one character's costume color impacts one or more other characters' colors. In some cases, you will see some dead ends. Your own preference for color combinations may differ from what I chose as my final point.

Example 1

Figures 14.17–14.20: An early 20th-century evening house party, with people dressed up at different levels of formality depending on their means. No overt color scheme was intended; the colors needed to harmonize without calling attention to themselves. Costumes were a combination of rented, pulled, and built pieces that needed to blend well.

The host and hostess are in the upper right corner and are older than the other characters. The characters in the lowest register may be considered the Main characters according to how you read the colors, but other viewers may decide that the middle register contains the Main characters.

The dress in the lowest register was changed from a day dress to an evening dress in order to support the evening dress worn by the woman at the far right. However, the light-colored evening dresses seemed less visually interesting than other costumes, and so more Intense colors were used in the final composition. This change necessitated substituting a black suit for the man on the right side of that register to balance the changes in the women's costumes. The colors of the other characters were also slightly reduced in Intensity to bring more focus to the characters in the lowest register.

FIGURE 14.17 Menswear filled in as a starting point

FIGURE 14.18 Women's wear added, with woman in the lowest register in a Green day dress

FIGURE 14.19   Dress in the lowest register was changed to an evening dress

FIGURE 14.20   A more Saturated color scheme for the two dresses in the lowest register make these costumes stand out more

Example 2

Figures 14.21–14.29: A late 18th- to early 19th-century rollicking comedy. An obvious Red/White/Blue color scheme was chosen to create a stylized impression. The costumes were a variety of pulled and built items.

The characters in the lowest register center were intended to be the Main characters, with comic relief in the center row right. Clever servants and citizens are in the center and upper registers.

When filling in the renderings, start with the neutrals that will be in the final color scheme, in order to fill up the blank spaces (Figure 14.21).

FIGURE 14.21   18th-century neutrals

As colors are added, relationships between characters are suggested or obscured. The first color, Red, is distributed throughout the costumes (Figure 14.22).

Adding Red to the woman's skirt in the lower left draws focus to this character (Figure 14.23).

Adding Red to the man's coat in the lower register creates a visual relationship with the woman next to this character and draws attention to both characters (Figure 14.24).

When a second major color is added, it can change the overall balance of the composition. In some cases, this will reveal the need for more of the first color on additional costumes to maintain its Dominant status.

FIGURE 14.22   Red is added to the neutrals

FIGURE 14.23   Red added

FIGURE 14.24 Red is moved to create a stronger relationship between the man and woman at the center of the lowest register

FIGURE 14.25 Blue, the Supporting color, is added to the costumes

In the groupings in Figures 14.26– 14.28, most of the characters' colors have been settled, but options for the main characters in the front row need to be explored before making final choices.

FIGURE 14.26 Blue replaces the Red on the men's coats

By changing the men's coats to Blue, the too-matched quality of Figure 14.24 is mitigated (Figure 14.26).

FIGURE 14.27 Variation with a low-Value Red on the central man's coat

Changing one coat to a lower-saturation Red diminishes the visual link with the woman in the Red dress that was present in Figure 14.24 and adds a less-stylized, more natural appearance to the color scheme (Figure 14.27).

FIGURE 14.28 Variation with Blue coat and dark Red skirt

This process may seem tedious, but it is helpful to try any combination that is in the back of your mind before deciding on a definite color scheme. When a designer is sure that they have considered all options, they can move forward with conviction in their choices.

FIGURE 14.29   The final color scheme

The final rendering in Figure 14.29 has the balance I was looking for. For a more stylized look, consider adding graphic Red, White, and Blue stripes as additional trim on the costumes.

Example 3

Figures 14.30–14.34: A 17th-century comedy of manners. The Main female character's costume and the wealthy men's coats were built pieces, blended with other items from stock that could be reworked and retrimmed.

The script mixed contemporary and 17th-century references, and the production was designed to mix the two periods. The director's intent was to play up the stylized comedy. Purple was chosen for the Main character, spread around throughout her admirers, and was Subdued for use as trim on the servants. The man in the dressing gown and the woman at the upper right were not part of the Main character's inner circle. The younger women in the center of the lowest register were part of this world, but were not as eager to curry favor with the main character as were the wealthy men.

FIGURE 14.30   Start with the Neutrals

FIGURE 14.31   Fill in the large areas of color

For this project, I found it easier to start with the Neutrals on the page in order to "work up" to the brighter costume colors that I knew I ultimately wanted to use.

Sashes, shirts, neckwear, and hosiery can all be areas in which to experiment with color, even on garments where the default color would be a very light Neutral for a realistic period production.

Ultimately, the final designs used light-colored hose in order to allow the added lace trim on the costumes to stand out. Large areas of off-white lace trim

FIGURE 14.32 Sashes and other accent colors added

FIGURE 14.33 Where one would expect white hose, experiment with adding colors

were used as the unifying element, to pull together the variety of colors on the costumes.

Summary

A unified color scheme creates a sense of unity within the production. Further, a tight costume color palette reduces the potential conflicts within the production design, as it is helpful to the lighting designer when they choose gel colors, and

FIGURE 14.34 Final result

to the scene designer when they mix paint colors. Take the time to experiment with color options before choosing the palette for a costume design, but be sure to work within that palette once it has been shared with the director and other designers. The goal for all designers should be a production that works as a whole, that supports the play and the production approach, and that communicates to the audience. Theatrical designers create a context in which the play unfolds before an audience. Done well, designs will enhance the audience's understanding of the characters and their world.

Color can be your magic weapon as a designer, as it is an element that people react to on a deep level. Because of color's power, use it to communicate with an audience and to enhance the production. Learn to use it with confidence, assurance, and joy, and your designs will be the better for it.

APPENDIX 1

Color Meanings

TABLE A1.1 Color meanings in East Asia Part 1

	Red	Pink	Orange	Yellow	Green	Blue	Purple
China (Feng Shui and Chinese Zodiac use color slightly differently)	Good luck Long life Weddings Celebrations Vitality Joy Wealth Summer Anger Fire Love Health	Good fortune Joy	Joy Weddings Self–Sacrifice Anger	Nourishment The Emperor Power Prosperity The Earth The Sacred Warmth (Pornographic publications in some parts of modern China)	New life Fertility Vitality Spring Harmony Growth Cleanliness Adultery and infidelity (green hats worn by the spouse of the adulterer or by prostitute)	Immortality Healing Trust Calm Wood Spring Growth Optimism	Mourning Misfortune Divinity Immortality Love and Romance
Japan	Life Love Energy Strength Passion Weddings Self–sacrifice Anger	Spring Youth Good Health	Courage Confidence Success Ignorance Love Happiness	Sun Brightness Energy Friendliness Happiness Irresponsibility Nature Caution Treachery Royalty Auspiciousness Buddha	Eternal Life Healing Money Growth Envy Freshness Restful Nature Vitality	Trust Intelligence Coldness Fidelity Calm Joy	Mourning Misfortune Divinity Immortality Love and Romance
Thailand/Burma	Buddha						Death Mourning Widows
Korea	Buddha					Immortality	

TABLE A1.2 Color meanings in East Asia Part 2

	White	Tan/beige	Grey	Brown	Black	Gold	Silver
China (Feng Shui and Chinese Zodiac use color slightly differently)	Death Mourning Age Autumn Purity Innocence Metal Bad luck		Dullness Humbleness Gloom	Misfortune	Evil Sadness Death Winter North Water Inauspicious Trust High quality	Glory Royalty Perfection Wisdom Good fortune Freedom from worldly cares	Purity Wealth
Japan	Death Mourning (white carnations) Purity Truth		Dreaminess	Earth Strength	Death Funerals Mystery Night Anger Gloom	Wealth Prestige	Precision Strength
Thailand/Burma	Purity Auspiciousness			Earth	Death Evil Bad luck Mystery		
Korea							

TABLE A1.3 Color meanings in West Asia, Part 1

	Red	Pink	Orange	Yellow	Green	Blue	Purple
India/Pakistan	Purity Power Fertility Sensuality Weddings Wealth Fire Married women Disruption (South India)	Very popular color for clothing Marriage Femininity (eastern India)	The most sacred color Courage Abstinence Death Rebellion	Peace Happiness Sacredness Merchants Commerce Meditation Auspicious	Hope Islam New beginnings Harvest Virtue Happiness Nature	Krishna Love Divine joy Truth Heavens Mercy Strength Bravery Manliness	Sorrow
West Asia	Danger Caution Evil		Mourning Loss	Prosperity Happiness Good fortune	Strength Fertility Prosperity Prestige Hope Spring Islam Perfect faith	Mourning Spirituality Protection Wealth Repelling evil	Mourning Wealth Nobility
Iran	Good fortune					Heaven Immortality Safety Protection Healing	
Turkey	Courage Death						
Israel					Bad news	Faith	

TABLE A1.4 Color meanings in West Asia, Part 2

	White	Beige/Tan	Grey	Brown	Black	Gold	Silver
India/Pakistan	Funerals Death Rebirth Widows Peace Purity Unhappiness			Mourning	Evil Darkness Anger Undesirable Laziness	Wealth Luxury Financial security	
West Asia	Purity Mourning			Earth Comfort	Death Evil Rebirth Mystery	Wealth	
Iran	Holiness Peace						
Turkey							
Saudi Arabia							
Israel							

TABLE A1.5 Color meanings in Africa and the Pacific, Part 1

	Red	Pink	Orange	Yellow	Green	Blue	Purple
Africa	Death Mourning Good luck in some areas of the continent			Highest-ranked people/ Royalty Wealth Ceremony Religion Mourning	Corruption (North Africa) Fertility		
Ethiopia							
Egypt	Good luck		Mourning	Mourning Soul Sun Happiness Prosperity Good fortune	Hope Spring Fertility	Truth Justice Virtue Faith Protection Reproduction	Virtue Faith
Nigeria	Royalty Power Aggression Vitality						
South Africa	Mourning	Poverty (Zulu)		Wealth	Death		
Pacific Islands							
Aboriginal Australia	Land Earth						
New Zealand	Nobility Divinity						
New Guinea							

TABLE A1.6 Color meanings in Africa and the Pacific, Part 2

	White	Beige/Tan	Grey	Brown	Black	Gold	Silver
Africa							
	Victory, Purity				Wisdom, Age, Maturity, Masculinity	Wealth	
Ethiopia	Illness, Purity				Impure, Unpleasant		
Egypt	Status				Rebirth		
Nigeria	Good luck, Peace				Ominous		
Zambia	Goodness, Cleanliness, Good luck						
South Africa	Goodness (Zulu)						
Pacific Islands							
Aboriginal Australia				The land	The people, Patriotic color		
New Zealand	Prosperity, Goodness		Mourning				
New Guinea	Cleanliness						

TABLE A1.7 Color meanings in Europe, Part 1

	Red	Pink	Orange	Yellow	Green	Blue	Purple
Europe	Love Danger Sexuality Stop Blood Sacrifice Masculinity	Baby girls Femininity Sensitivity Love Romance	Halloween Harvest Purity Cleanliness Autumn	Love Joy Hope Energy Cowardice Hazards Happiness Weakness	Spring New life Christmas (with Red) Good luck Nature Jealousy Money	Tradition Calm Christ Virgin Mary Reliability Truth Fidelity	Royalty Mourning Luxury Power Vanity
France	Passion Love Lust Vitality		Earth	Summer Joy Jealousy	Earth	Water Reliability Trust	Freedom Peace
Germany							
UK	Power Authority			Envy		Depression Right wing/ Conservatism	
Ireland			Protestantism		Catholicism National color St. Patrick		
Netherlands/Belgium	Nature Government	Baby boys (Belgium)	Dutch Royal Family (Netherlands)	Food		Baby girls (Belgium)	

Italy	Light Fidelity		Death Mourning Nobility Beauty
Greece		Strength	
Ukraine			Sadness Hospitality Benevolence
Russia	Communism Weddings		

TABLE A1.8 Color meanings in Europe, Part 2

	White	Beige/Tan	Grey	Brown	Black	Gold	Silver
Europe	Weddings Spirituality Angels Purity Peace Medical Antiseptic Neutrality Surrender	Boring		Earth Rustic Humbleness	Death Evil Mourning Elegance Formality Magic	Wealth High Quality Status	Purity Preciousness
France	Purity				Sophistication Elegance		
Germany							
UK			Foggy	Dependable Earthy Wholesome			
Ireland	Leisure						
Nether-lands/Belgium							
Italy	Virtue Purity Death (white carnations)				Death Widows Mourning Humility		
Greece							
Ukraine							
Russia							

TABLE A1.9 Color meanings in the Americas, Part 1

	Red	Pink	Orange	Yellow	Green	Blue	Purple
Americas	Love Danger Anger Passion Stop		Energy Vitality Creativity Autumn Harvest	Happiness Hope Creativity Energy Warning Weakness	Regeneration Luck Environment Jealousy Go	Trust Peace Sadness Masculine Conservative	Royalty Spirituality Faith Fame Luxury
US/Canada	Love Sexuality Christmas (with Green) Valentine's day Conservatism (US) Communism	Cuteness Sweet Feminine	Halloween Harvest	Cowardice Warning	Money Freshness Nature Spring Environment Olive green (military)	Liberalism (US) Authority Heritage Business Loyalty	Artistic Unusual Luxury Royalty Wealth Honor
First Nations America	East Success War Day Earth Peace Happiness Wounds Thunder			Up above Sun Dawn Day	Center Plants Earth Rain Summer	North Trouble Defeat Sky Water Sadness Female	

(Continued)

TABLE A1.9 Continued

	Red	Pink	Orange	Yellow	Green	Blue	Purple
Mexico	Blood Religion (with white)				Independence Hope		
Nicaragua							
Peru							
Brazil					Death Mourning	Mourning Trust Serenity	Death Mourning

TABLE A1.10 Color meanings in the Americas, Part 2

	White	Beige/Tan	Grey	Brown	Black	Gold	Silver
Americas	Weddings Spirituality Angels Purity Peace Cleanliness Elegance Medical			Comfort Stability Organic Poverty		Power Wealth Exclusivity High quality	
US/Canada	Wedding Cleanliness Chic Quiet	Basic Vanilla Boring	Indistinct Boring Old Depression	Earthy Natural Dirt	Death Funerals Corruption Hidden Sophisticated		
First Nations America	South Winter Death Snow Peace Happiness			Plants Earth Summer Rain Down below	West Night Cold Male Disease Death		
Mexico	Unity Catholicism Purity						
Nicaragua Columbia				Disapproval Discouragement			
Peru					Mourning Color for male clothing		
Brazil	Angels Health			Nature	Sophistication Religion Authority		

APPENDIX 2

Period Color Schemes

Color ideas for a specific time period can be deduced from a variety of sources. Portraits and paintings, photographs, advertisements, fashion plates and magazines, tapestries, historic garments, home interiors, architecture, decorative arts such as floor tiles or mosaics or frescos or pottery, and other sources **from the period that you are researching** are useful inspiration for creating a color scheme. Somewhat less useful are secondary sources, such as collections of redrawn images from original sources, including Owen Jones's survey of historic ornament, Racinet's survey of historic European costume, and other similar compendiums.

When looking at historic sources, also note whether the colors are in direct contact with one another or whether there are black and/or white borders between hues, whether the colors interlock or are adjacent, and the relative clarity and value of the hues. Listed below are summaries of colors from both primary and secondary sources. Doing your own research is always best, but these examples will give you a quick starting point.

China – traditional	Red, Metallic Gold, Bronze, Black, Jade, Grey Blue, Golden Yellow, White, Red Brown, Indigo, Deep Berry, Rose, Grey-Green, Apple Green, Rose Red
Japan – traditional	Red, Deep and Faded Indigo, Off-White, Golden Yellow, Black, Rust Red, Jade Green, Rose, Buff, Pale Greys, Pale Blue
India/Pakistan – traditional	Bright Pink, Red, Ochre, Tan, Pink, Jade Green, Mint Green, Yellow, Lapis Blue, Fuchsia, Blue-Green, Cool Blue, Orange-Red, Saffron Yellow, Indigo, Turmeric Orange-Yellow, Dark Green-Black, Red, Metallic Gold, Golden Yellow, White, Black
	Blue – Krishna, Yellow – Vishnu, Red – Lakshmi

(*Continued*)

(Continued)

Ancient Mesopotamia	Deep Tile Blue, Golden Tan, Deep Red Brown, Medium Grass Green, Clay
Persia/traditional Iran	Buff, Blue Green, Silver, Bronze, Metallic Gold, Ochre Gold, Black, Golden Yellow, Rose, Buff Pink, Brown, Carmine Red, Red, Tile Blue, Deep Indigo, Jade, Pale and Deep Spring Green
Turkey – traditional	Red Madder, Indigo, Warm Tan, Black, Metallic Gold, Deep Turquoise Blue
Ancient Egypt	Tan, Lapis Blue, White, Soft Red, Rust, Clay, Bronze, Lotus Green, Ochre Gold, Metallic Gold, Black
North Western Africa – traditional	Metallic Gold, Deep Cool Tile Blue, Deep Blue-Green, Red-Brown, Carmine Red, White, Off-White, Jade Green, Soft Orange, Deep Cream, Green
North Africa – traditional	Black, Rust, Red, Red-Brown, Golden Ochre, Dark Brown, Red, White, Yellow
Central Western and Eastern Africa – traditional	Black, Rust, Red, Red-Brown, Golden Ochre, Dark Brown, Red, White, Yellow, Black and White together, Saffron Orange, Leaf Green, Sky Blue, Straw Golden Beige, Bright Golden Yellow
First Nations America – traditional	Softened Red, White, Brown, Yellow, Green, Black, Blue, Tan, Clay Red, Cream
South America – traditional	Clay, Black, Cream, Tan, Brick Red, Red, Blue, Yellow, Brown and Cream, Red and Pink, Light and Dark Blue, White, Grey, Brown, Tawny Orange, Vivid Pink, Orange, Vivid Blue, Purple, Golden Yellow, Blue, Vibrant Green, Black, Royal Blue
Ancient Greece	Buff Tan, Black, Red Clay/Terra-Cotta, Cream, Deep Tile Blue, Grey, Golden Ochre, Some Soft Green, Yellow, Purple accents
Ancient Rome	Off-White, White, Carmine Red, Rust Red, Black, Ochre, Deep Blue, Blue-Grey, Green, Purple, Purplish Brown, Metallic Gold
Byzantine Empire/ Turkey–Italy	Metallic Gold, Medium Blue, Black, Bronze, Grass Green, Tan, Indigo Blue, Carmine Red, Natural Beige, Golden Yellow, Purple, Pearl White
Medieval Europe	Brown, Rust Red, Cool Red, Tan, Cream, Dull Green, Ochre Gold, Dull Blue, Sky Blue, Black, Ultramarine Blue, Dark Blue, Burgundy, Soft Green, Soft Grey, Soft Orange, Rose, Pink, Gold, Blue with Yellow, Terra-Cotta with Green
Renaissance Italy	Buff, Tan, Pale Grey, Blue-Grey, Bronze Green, Medium Green, Medium Blue, Rose Red, Soft Rose, Soft Orange, Aqua, Dull Burgundy, Black, Off-White, Clay, Carmine Red, Ochre Gold, Rust Red, Warm Brown, Lapis Blue, Dark Warm Brown, Gold, Yellow, Copper Green, Softened Blue-Green, Sage, Copper, Buff Rose, Metallic Gold

(Continued)

(*Continued*)

Elizabethan Britain	Red, White, Metallic Gold, and Black are key colors. Buff, Tan, Soft Brown, Medium Green, Dull Burgundy, Rose, Sky Blue, Deep Blue, Copper Red, Grey, Pearl White
16th-century Europe	Celery Green, Lavender, Gold, Ochre Gold, Tan, Medium Green, Grass Green, Black, White, Beige, Rosy Pink, Tile Blue, Soft Orange, Red, Dark Burgundy, Metallic Gold
17th-century Europe	Metallic Gold, White, Blue, Golden Yellow, Rust Brown, Soft Grey, Pale Grey Green, Bronze Green, Soft Pink, Buff, Dull Dark Blue-Black, accents of Soft Green, Peach, and Rose
18th–century Europe	Warm Tan, Buff, Metallic Gold, Brick Red, Dull Green/Grey-Green, Wedgewood Blue, Rose, Pale Yellow, Pale Blue, Blue Green, Off-White, Ochre, Pale Buff, Copper Green Pale and Medium, Pale Avocado, Rose Buff, Pale Grey, Golden Yellow, White, Dark Brown, Geranium, Mint, Straw, Grey, Black
1790–1800s Europe/the "Empire" Era	Revival of Pompeian colors plus the sense of Classical monuments in White Marble. Military influences. Buff, Metallic Gold, Tan, Crimson, White, Purple or Mauve, Yellow, Black, Soft Pinks, Green, Navy, Red
19th-century Europe overall	Tobacco Brown, Brick Red, Crimson, Bottle Green, Plum, Dark Green, Blue, Cream, Burgundy, Aniline Purple, Deep Rust Red, sprigs and stripes
1800–10 Europe and North America	White, Cream, Buff, Tan, Grey Brown, Black, Red, Soft Rose Pink, Pale Yellow, Blue, Green or Purple accents, Gold accessories, sprigged and embroidered fabrics Men in Black, Brown, Grey, Buff, Navy, White shirts, and dark Red accents
1810s Europe and North America	White, Muslin, Pale Grey-White, Linen, Black, Gold trim and accessories, Yellow, Lilac, Primrose, Green, Sky Blue, Blonde Lace, Scarlet, Violet, Blush Pink, Taupe, Blue-Grey, Grass Green, Mauve. Sprigs and stripes, embroidery Men in Black, Brown, Grey, Buff, Navy, White shirts, and dark Red accents
1820s Europe and North America	Muslin, White, Pink, Pale Blue, Lavender, Spring Green, Red, Black, Metallic Gold trim, Violet, Olive Green, Smoke Grey, Milky Brown, Pale Yellow, Tan, Cream, Grey-Green. Becoming brighter over the decade with Geranium Pink Red, Clay, Rust Red, Warm Lavender, Green, Sunflower Yellow, Sky Blue, Cobalt Blue Men in stripes, checks, large open plaids, solids. Black, Brown, Grey, Buff, Navy, White shirts, Dark Green, Deep Blue, Brown, and Burgundy, dark Red accents. Color on vests, neckties and accessories

(*Continued*)

(*Continued*)

1830s Europe and North America	Stone, Straw, Brick, Honey Brown, Blonde Lace, Tan, Slate Grey, Dark Grey, Rose, Green, Creamy Yellow, Tile Red, Brown, Fawn, Black, Yellow, Blue, Blue and Black with Red and Green hints, Lilac, Pale Blue, Blue. Printed patterns on fabric becoming more important. Colors beginning to be more subdued over the second part of the decade. Brown, Violet, Dark Blue, Green, Rose, Pigeon Grey, Dark Rose, Blues, Secondary and Tertiary colors in diminished tones Men in stripes, bold checks, large plaids, solids. Dark Green, Deep Blue, Brown, Greys, Blacks, and Burgundy. Color on vests, neckties and accessories
1840s Europe and North America	Secondary and Tertiary Colors, shot silk colors of two tones, print dress fabrics, plaids. Combinations of colors in garments worn together, such as dresses and shawls or mantles and gloves. All Cool or Warm Colors such as Lilac and Myrtle Green, Drab Grey-Brown with Ruby Red, and Green and Rose Pink. Light Green, Soft Pink, Lilac, White, Lilac, Crimson, Light Blue, Pale Green, Lavender and Cherry Red Shot Fabrics, Dark Blue, Black, Grey, Beige, Brown, Pink Grey, Violet and Green, Dark Blue, Dark Green, Brown, Copper, and Burgundy Men in bold checks, large plaids, solids. Dark Green, Deep Blue, Brown, Greys, Blacks, and Burgundy. Color on vests, neckties and accessories
1850s Europe and North America	Blue, Fawn, White, Blonde lace, Blue, Evergreen, Brown, Yellow, Cream, Blue-Grey, Terra-Cotta Red, Navy, Wedgewood Blue, Emerald, Chestnut, Dark Blue, Maroon, Ocher Gold, Cerise, Scarlet, Pink, Sky Blue, Claret, Green, Lavender, Pink, Lilac, Green, and Black Contrasting Stronger Colors: Brown and Rose, Mauve and Purple, Blue and White, Green and Lilac, Straw with Mauve, Sapphire, Light and Dark Green with Purple and Grey and Black, Dark and Light Rose with Lavender and Ruby Red, Green with Brown and Blue, Yellow with Green and Lavender, Brown and Mauve, Light Purple with Light Green, Pink and Mauve, Blue with Light Green, Light Purple with Light Green, Bright Green with Poppy Red, Yellow and White and Pink. Horizontal trim on skirts Plaid, often with wide stripes of color in plaids. "Turkish" and military style influences Men in Black, Greys, some Browns, Plaids, with Burgundy, Navy and Deep Green. Menswear with strong plaids, checks, stripes, and patterns for jackets, vests, and trousers, sometimes in contrasting surface patterns

(*Continued*)

(Continued)

1860s Europe and North America	Sharper colors of Purple, Red, and Green made possible with aniline dyes. Contrasting Colors: Magenta, Clay Red, Gold Braid, Scarlet, White, Cream, Deep Green, Medium Blue, Aniline dye-based colors, Black, Warm Brown, Mauve, Violet Blue, Black and White, Grey and Pink, Blue and White with Green, Brown with Blue, Brown with Mauve, Grey, Drab Brown, Cerise, Bronze Green with Drab, Ruby Red, White, Buff, Green and Violet, Maize and Purple. Plum, Wood Rose, Turquoise, Brown, Grass Green, Tile Blue, Bismarck Brown, Ophelia Garnet, Ruby, Plum, Marine Blue, Vesuvius Red, Nile Green, Chocolate. Colored shoes for women
	Men in Black, Greys, some Browns, Plaids, with Burgundy, Navy and Deep Green, with medium to small plaids, checks, stripes, and patterns for jackets, vests, and trousers, sometimes in contrasting surface patterns
1870s Europe and North America	Buttercup Yellow, Bottle Blue-Green, Crimson, Maroon, Purple, Black, Dark Blue, Red, Deep Blackened Green, Grey-Green, Brick Red, Cream, Dull Soft Orange, Navy, Dark Green and Grey, Pale Blue-Grey, Pink, Apple Green, Pink, Violet Olive, Dove Grey, Light Brown, Maroon, Green, Ecru, Black, Sea Green, Reds, Dark Green, Warm Brown, Myrtle Green, Violet, Mauve, Nile Green, Plum, Chestnut, Maize, Fawn, Brown, White, Grey-Brown. Grey, Black
	Grey with Black, solid Black with Black and White stripes, Pink with Sky Blue, Blue-Grey and Pink, Salmon and Green, Black over Light Colors, Yellow or Blue-Green trimmed in Blue, Moss Green with Pale Blue, Deep Violet and Blue Grey, Blue and Green, Almond with Chestnut, Light Blue and Moss Green, Dark Blue with Crimson, Bronze and Cream, Dark and Light Green, Plum with Cardinal Red, Pale Blue and Peacock, Salmon Pink and Brown, Olive and Cream, Blue and Green over Bronze Green, Canary Yellow with Blue, Brown and Pink, Coral and Green, Blue and Green, Violet and Mandarin Orange, Blue and Scarlet, Blue and Pink, Prune and Pink, Bronze and Blue, Fawn with Sage or Olive Green, Olive and Turquoise, Pearl Grey and Pink, Nile Green and Black, Bronze and Old Gold, Claret and Pink, Claret and Pale Blue. Browns for women's street wear. Coffee-color lace. Outline trimmings around edges of garments, trim may be lighter than the garment itself. Light and Dark tones of the same hue popular on one costume, often with the upper areas of the ensemble lighter than the lower. Stripes more common than plaids
	Men wear Black and Grey, checks, subtle plaids, solids. Color on neckties and small accessories

(Continued)

(*Continued*)

1880s Europe and North America	The return of shot silk to fashion. Heliotrope and Light Green, Heliotrope and Apricot, Olive and Blue, Pink with Black, Lavender and Yellow, Peacock Blue with Nile Green, Strong Red, and Soft Green. Greyed Pale Green, White, Deep Maroon, Dark Brown, Deep Blue, Ocher Orange, Pale Pink, Mauve, Pale Yellow, Heliotrope, Blue, Bottle Green, Claret, Cardinal Red, Raspberry, Red-Brown, Cardinal Red, Brown, Green, Dark Blue, Claret, Deep Ruby. Summer colors include Heliotrope, Bronze, Terra-Cotta, Peacock Blue, Grey, Orange, Jonquil, Dull Green, Brown and Crimson, Brown and Green, Pink and Bright Yellow, Salmon and Ruby, Cardinal Red and Dark Blue, Shrimp and Olive, Rifle Green, Grey and Pink, Peach, Old Rose, Sea Green, Ecru and Blue. Some brighter colors coming in to compete with electric lighting in ballrooms. Woolens and Velvets combined in ensembles
	Men in Greys, Blacks, Buffs, and Tans with checks, subtle plaids, and solids. Most color on neckties and small accessories
1890s Europe and North America	Pale Blue women's evening wear. Violet, Mauve, Black and White, Flamingo, Coral, Red, Yellow, Lettuce Green and Pearl Grey, Pale Green, Heliotrope, White, Deep Green, Blue, Ochre, Mauve, Plum, Lavender and Purple, White, Prussian Blue, Ochre Gold, Rust Red, Maroon, Sycamore Green, Petunia, Orchid Purple, Azalea Red, Sunflower Yellow, Maize, Leaf Brown, Electric Blue, Turquoise Blue, Amethyst, Violet, Cornflower Blue, Olive Green, Yellow, Dark Blue, Navy, Deep Red, Black Satin, Camel Tan, Black, Old Rose, Greyed Periwinkle, Butter, Ecru, Cream, Cornflower Blue, Green, Grey-Blue, Brown
	Bolder colors on the upper half of the body such as a Plum bodice with a Black skirt, Red bolero over a Black bodice. Shot silk returns as well as colored chiffon over different-colored silk to create a shot silk effect. Heliotrope shot with Blue, shot Apricot with Mushroom Velvet, Mauve and Light Green, Steel Blue and Pink, Burnt Sienna and Emerald, Myrtle Green and Cerise, Moss Green and Red, Red and Pink, Green and Pink, Blue and Violet, Pale Peach and Pale Green, Pink and Black, Brown and Black, Yellow with Pale Green and Pink, Lilac and Pale Blue, Lilac with Green, Green with Black, Lemon with Blue and Pink, Navy with Gold and Red, Arsenic Green and Black, Olive and Blackened Navy, Salmon and Cream, Lavender and Olive
	Japanese-inspired patterns are popular. More sportswear for women. Colors were often sharply discordant with sleeves of one color against a bodice of another hue. Broad stripes of Red and Blue or Ecru and Brown. More emphasis on the bodice as the skirt becomes simpler as compared with the 1880s
	Men in Greys, Blacks, Buffs, and Tans, with checks, subtle plaids, and solids. Color on neckties and small accessories

(*Continued*)

(Continued)

1900s Europe and North America	Mauve, Lavender, Soft Blue, Rose, Grey, Cream, Tan, Navy, Black, Soft Clay Red, Black edging, White, Buff, Linen, Soft Berry, Dark Grey Green, Khaki, Lilac and Purple, Pale Aqua with Buff Pink and Pale Blue-Grey, Medium Blue and Navy, Navy and White, Copper and Dark Brown
	Men in Black, Grey, Buff, Cream, Tan
1910s Europe and North America	Ballets Russes "Exotic" influences – Orange, Maroon, Red, Scarlet, Bright Blue, Deep Golden Yellow, Blue-Green, Raspberry, Plum, Emerald, Sapphire. Sienna, Cream, Malachite Green, Sky Blue, White
	Also, White garments with brighter Sashes and with over-gowns. Sheer overlays of lace and chiffon in contrasting colors with solid edging. Cutwork lace, floral appliques. Tabards. Military and sailor accents. Edge banding. Floral prints, subtle stripes, and plaids
	Men in Black, Grey, Cream, Buff, Tan, Taupe, Browns, Navy, solid and striped shirts with White collars
1920s Europe and North America	Black becomes a fashion color for women outside of mourning. White, Cream, Tan, Ochre, Blue, Gold, Turquoise, Jade, Bright and Deep Reds, Orange, Brilliant Blue, Deep Cucumber Green, Bright Color with Black against a Cream Background, Secondary and Tertiary Colors, Soft Lime, Purple, Greys, Buffs, Copper
	Embroidery, vertical elements in center of dresses, tiered skirts, beading, appliqués. Geometrics and stylized florals. Egyptian, Chinese, Asian, and Russian influences. Tulle and Georgette worn over silk slips. Silk velvets. Borders that break up the large geometric areas of bodices and skirts
	Men in Black, Grey, Navy, Brown, Off-White, Red and Burgundy accents, Tan, Buff, Blue, White collars
1930s Europe and North America	Toned-down colors of Orange, Periwinkle Blue, Spruce Green, Golden Ochre, Maroon, Dark Brown, Black, White. Strong or Dusty pastels such as Pink, Yellow, Sea Green, White, Cream, Black, Red, Magenta, Coral, Lavender, Gold, Grey
	Shaped seams with crepe, georgette, bias, wool crepe, rayon, soft wool. Satin for evening, especially in White
	Men in Brown, Olive, Grey, Navy, less Black. Burgundy Green and Red accents
1940s Europe and North America	Early – Coral, Lime, Pearl Grey, Khaki Tan, Olive Green, Reds, Blues, Denim, Dark Green, Brown, Grey, Black
	Later – Pink, Grey, Blue, Cream, Lavender, Rose, Turquoise, Reds, Black

(Continued)

(Continued)

1950s Europe and North America	Bright and Pale Pink, Grey, Pale Blue, Yellow, Lavender, Turquoise, Sea Green, Mint, Peach, Cream, Black, Greyed Purple, Candy Pink and Mint Green, Yellow with Blue and Silver, or Yellow with Brown-Red and Green. Black, Salmon, Copper, Dark Green
1960s Europe and North America	Brighter pastels to acid colors. Red, Lavender, Gold, Coral, Emerald, Pinks with Gold, Blue with Brown, Green with Coral, Black and White, Orange with Grass Green
1970s Europe and North America	Denim Blue, Red, Black, Peach, Cream, Beige, Brown, Rust, Dark Green, Neutralized and Faded Pure Colors, Red/White/Blue combinations in the US, Black, Silver, Red, Avocado, Old Gold, Burgundy and Pink
1980s Europe and North America	Olive, Brown, Black, Indigo, Maroon, Pink, Turquoise, Bright Purple, Orange/Purple/Teal combinations, Hot Pink, Neon Green and Yellow accents, Faded Denim Blue
1990s Europe and North America	Black, Grey, Red, Indigo, White, Cream, Pink, Teal, Bright Yellow, Bright Green, Denim Blue
2000s Europe and North America	Black, Metallic Gold, White, Camel, Tan, Cordovan, Blue, Denim Blue, Indigo, Red, Purple, Teal, Turquoise, Aqua
2010s Europe and North America	Black, Green, Blue, Denim Blue, Indigo, Red, Purple, Camel, Tan, Grey, Burgundy, Deep Pink, Yellow, Soft Grey Blue, Red-Brown

APPENDIX 3

Lighting Design for Costume Designers

Light and Color are intrinsically bound together. Therefore, it is important for a costume designer to understand the basic science of light in order to predict how light will affect costume colors and to successfully communicate with a lighting designer.

In our atmosphere, there are forms of energy that travel in waves. The electromagnetic spectrum measures the waves, which range from X-rays through Ultraviolet to Infrared and radio waves. In the middle of the range is the Visible Spectrum, a group of waves of a length that humans can see. When the waves, generated by a light source, hit an object, they can either be absorbed or reflected into our eyes. The rods and cones in our eyes receive the waves that are reflected by a surface and transmit them into our brain, which interprets the waves as color. Each of the waves in the visible spectrum is a color in a range from dark Red through Violet.

A lighting source sends out waves that are either absorbed or reflected by fabric. For Theatre, we start with White light from a theatrical fixture with roughly the same amount of all the color waves. The different light waves will be absorbed or reflected by different fabric colors. For example, with an Orange fabric, the Blue contained within White light would be absorbed, and the Orange would be reflected so that we can see the Orange color.

Instruments

White light is considered the starting point for all lighting. However, because of the mechanical differences in how instruments emit light, the colors of the light they create will differ somewhat. An incandescent lamp has a glowing filament, and so it has more Red and Orange tones than other types of instruments, and the light emitted appears more Yellowed. Florescent lamps have more of a Blue-Green cast. LED fixtures have light-emitting diodes that turn on in various groupings, and their White light appears slightly Blue. Different companies use different groupings in their LED products. Automatic fixtures with arc lamps are slightly bluer than LEDs.

Different types of instruments will emit different qualities of light. Because light is so tied to the inventory of equipment that the theatre owns, and because lighting terminology may not be familiar to the costume designer, here is a quick summary of what the lighting designer may be using:

- Blinders: Instruments that are pointed at the audience in order to obscure their view of the stage. Used for scene changes when there is not a front curtain, for special effects, or for rock shows.
- Borders/strip lights: Strip lights give a large amount of color coverage with a rack of lights that can be gelled in multiple colors and cover an expanse of the stage. Often used on a cyclorama, either casting light from below or above, or as footlights at the front edge of the stage floor. These may be incandescent or LED instruments.
- Cyc lights: As the name implies, these instruments tend to be used on the cyclorama, the large scenic backdrop in the theatre. They create a large, even expanse of light, and can be hung at the bottom or top of a cyc. The light tends to be sharp, so they may be gelled with a softly frosted gel in order to soften the light with or without adding other colors. These may be incandescent or LED instruments.
- Effect lights: These are specialty instruments that can be used to create a special effect or to add to the scenic impression. The instruments include scanners, video panels, moving lights, or laser lights.
- Ellipsoidals (or Lekos): Ellipsoidals are some of the most standard instruments in the lighting designer's toolkit. They create a crisp-edged cone of light that falls onto the stage. This edge may be softened with a frosted gel. The instrument has a long cylindrical shape. Different degree sizes of instruments will create a different degree of light beam, and variable zoom ellipsoidals will allow more choice in the size of the projected illumination. The size of the light circle projected onstage and the distance the instrument is hung away from the stage surface are the two most important factors in working with these instruments. These factors may also determine at what intensity the instrument is run, which will have an effect on the color of light that is cast, with or without an added gel. These may be incandescent or LED instruments.
- Follow spots: A spotlight directs audience attention by adding extra light to a performer, making everything else onstage appear a little darker and duller. A show will often require two spotlight operators in order to cover two main performers. These instruments are often used for musicals, opera, and

concerts. Follow spots project a very bright light that may be gelled, which can also flatten out details on costumes and faces.

- Fresnels: This is one of the most basic and reliable instruments available. A fresnel casts a soft-edged circle of light that can change size. The soft-edged light may be sharpened by adding a "shutter" or "barn door" to create a crisp edge. These instruments have a "stepped" or grooved lens and tend to be taller and wider than they are long. The smaller the diameter of the lens on the instrument, the smaller the size and intensity of the light beam. These may be incandescent or LED instruments.

- LED units: LED or light emitting diode instruments are more versatile than standard incandescent units. The diodes inside the instruments give a designer the ability to mix colors, from saturated to subtle. Colors may be changed quickly, both within a production and while setting levels during technical rehearsals. The intensity of the light emitted allows for units to be run at a low-power setting, although that can also affect the color of the light emitted.

- Moving lights: As their name implies, moving lights can move around the axis of their mounting point, which allows the location, texture, sharpness, and color of the light they emit to change during a performance.

- Par Cans: Par Cans are a parabolic aluminum reflector (Par) that is contained in a fixture (Can). They create a wash of light. There are variations in the width of the light beam produced as well as the shape, ranging from circular to oval. These instruments come in a variety of shapes and may hold incandescent or LED lamps. The classic incandescent Par Can has a smooth barrel that is longer than it is wide and looks a bit like a gallon paint can. This is an old-style fixture that is being phased out.

- UV black lights: These instruments give an unworldly glow to a dark scene and add an interesting violet tone to regular lighting. Black light will make white fabrics appear to glow in the dark.

- Work lights: Work lights are used for simple illumination onstage, commonly during rehearsals. These instruments do not emit glamorous light. A lighting designer may choose work lights for a scene in which pretensions and magic are stripped away. The light emitted tends to be flat and is not particularly flattering to skin tones or to costume colors.

Color and Lights

Primary Colors are the three to four basic or fundamental hues that are used to mix additional colors. Lighting primaries are Red, Blue, and Green. Lighting is mixed using Additive color, in which the primaries are combined to make a full range of colors. Using all three colors together in equal measures should result in a pure white light.

Color is added to the light beam with gels or with the diodes in LED instruments. Gels or diodes take out all of the colors that occur naturally in white light

except for the color of the added gel or programmed diode. (For simplicity's sake, from this point I will refer to colored light as being gelled, no matter how the color is created.) Combining different-colored beams of light will create Additive mixing, by adding in more light colors in the area where different colored lights overlap on the stage. For example, by adding a second instrument with a Red gel to a lighting area that is also lit with a Blue gel, there is Additive mixing where the two pools of light overlap, and the Red and Blue lights would create Magenta where they mix. If a third instrument with a Green gel is added to this mix, White light would be created in the overlap of the three lights, with secondary lighting colors of Yellow, Magenta, and Blue-Green in the other overlaps.

It is common to use Blue and Amber side lights to theoretically produce a White light on the stage. If the lamps were equal in age and power, the mix would be complete and would result in clear white light. However, the mix often is not absolutely complete, and, because incandescent instruments are naturally slightly Red/Orange, there is always a warm cast to the color created by gelled incandescent instruments onstage. As a result, a Red- or Amber-gelled light beam will tend to appear even Warmer than the gel color itself may indicate. Colored light created by LED diodes, which naturally tend towards a Blue cast, will appear slightly Bluer than the diode may indicate.

The pigment primaries that costume designers tend to use in painting and dyeing are Red, Blue, and Yellow. Because lighting and costume designers conceptualize color mixing from two very different perspectives, it is good to know the basics of both systems in order to understand and communicate better. Pigments are considered Subtractive colors, as mixing colors reduces the Purity of each hue and creates a Neutralized (mixed with its complement) and/or Subdued color (intensity reduced by being mixed with another color). If all three pigment primary colors are mixed equally, the result should be Black. Each pigment absorbs wavelengths, and the result of the mixed color is that the **only hues reflected are those that the pigments do not absorb**. The further away on the color wheel the pigment colors that are mixed are located from one another, the more wavelengths are absorbed and the more Subdued the colors, up to the point where Complements are mixed to create a truly Neutralized color.

As discussed earlier, the instruments themselves add a color cast and/or a roundness or flatness to the light they emit. Age of lamps, type of instrument, and brand of instrument will all affect the resulting color onstage, outside of the added color diode or gel choices. Colors in lighting fixtures are usually considered to be unsaturated, but they still affect the colors onstage.

A regular incandescent fixture emits light with a Yellow cast. **In addition, the lower the intensity at which the instrument is run, the Yellower the light will appear, even without a gel added.** This is important to know, as instruments are often run at much lower intensities than 100%, and so the light they emit is inherently Yellowed. Add a warm-colored gel to an incandescent light and the resulting light projected on the stage will be quite warm. For Nostalgic or

Period shows, an Amber gel is often added to the instruments. As the gel reduces the color that is projected, and the instrument produces light that is already somewhat warm, an Amber gel on an instrument that is running at below 100% intensity will play havoc with a Blue costume because there is little Blue in the light beam emitted. Therefore, the Blue costume will look flatter and duller than the costume designer may expect. In the same situation, Yellow garments will appear more yellow, skin tones will be more orange than in real life, and details can be lost. However, if the set is painted in warm wood tones, it may be enhanced by this situation. Because lighting designers tend to determine their lighting levels on an empty set and to respond to the colors that the set has been painted, be mindful to let the lighting designer know what colors you have chosen for the costumes and how you would like them to appear.

In a small theatre, the audience is closer, and the lighting grid may be lower, and so the lights tend to be run at less-than-full intensity. This tends to result in a definite Amber shift in the color of the light emitted. In a larger house with a proscenium stage, the instruments are further away from the actors and tend to be run at higher intensity, even for night scenes, and so the light color will be less Amber than in a smaller theatre.

More Saturated lighting colors are used in certain situations, such as non-realistic productions, sunrise and sunset, night, candle- or lantern-light, light filtered through gobos, forests, rock and roll shows, and scenes with a background area that is not supposed to be featured, contrasted with a brighter and less-colorful acting area. If the lighting designer is talking about using Saturated gel colors, have a conversation about which colors and fabrics you are using and about the result that you are hoping for onstage.

Here are a few commonly used gel or gel-equivalent colors in LED lights, with their effects on costume colors:

- Amber: an Orangey Yellow, this gel can flatten out color and texture.
- Straw: a less intense version of Amber, it will add warmth without as much "muddiness" as Amber.
- Surprise Pink: has a cool feel, may help counteract the amber in the lights.
- No-color Blue: makes a cooler, cold effect. The effect becomes Grey when being used at a lower lighting intensity because of the inherent Yellowness that the instrument produces in this situation.
- Deep Blue-Violet down light: can add excitement to the look of the garment.

Adding a saturated or lower-value tone from LED instruments can add more depth to the overall look when combined with a mix of higher-value gel colors.

For colors in costumes, **it is better to have a tighter palette to get a more uniformly positive look under colored lights**. For a wide range of costume colors and textures, higher-value or sheer color gels will give a better overall effect. Also, don't pick low-intensity, tired costume colors unless you want the costume to fade. Mauve, Lavender, Taupe, and other greyed pale tones are colors that generally wash out onstage under lights, as well as making many Caucasian skin tones look tired and dull. At the same time, Black fabrics (and wigs) can appear to be different colors under stage lights depending on fiber content, which can complicate matters if you are trying to match Blacks in a costume. Remember, if the costumes have a wide range of colors, there are going to be scenes where at least some of the colors are diminished, especially if the lighting designer is inspired to use a wide range of intense gels.

Be aware also of the scale of your prints and details, as they can get lost on the stage. Use deliberate patterns and textures, or accept that a small print will appear as a background texture rather than as a visible pattern.

Direction of Light

The angles of the light that falls on an actor will not necessarily alter the costume colors, but the effect of lighting angles is worth mentioning.

Light in nature often comes from above, but theatre light can come from the front, straight down, the sides, at an angle from above, the back, and up from the stage floor. Ideally, the variety of lighting angles will give an overall rounded effect that will show off the textures and volume of the garments.

- Front-light illuminates actors and their faces and fills out some of the shadows that result from other lighting angles, but can also flatten out some dimensional details.
- Down-light or top-light will cast shadows from hairstyles and hats onto faces and show off the folds in garments. Down-light adds texture but also shows every unwanted garment wrinkle. Many lighting designers use more Saturated colors in their down-lights.
- Strong side-light shows off the shape of bodies and garments, enhancing a three-dimensional effect. Dance lighting often primarily uses side-light in order to show off the dancer's shapes. Strong side-light often necessitates lighting instruments being placed in the theatre wings, which is something to be factored in if there will be a quick costume change during a production – beware of traffic patterns and hot lights on light trees.
- Angled light from above is very common in theatre lighting and combines some of the properties of front-, side-, and down-light.
- Back-light helps visually separate actors from the background, which is helpful in keeping the actors visible when the scenery and costume colors are similar.
- Footlights will counteract some facial shadows on older performers and wrinkles in costumes. This light coming up from the floor can also appear odd, because the shadows fall up, rather than down as our eyes expect from nature. Footlights can be used to create a stylized effect that harkens back to their use in theatre prior to the use of overhead electric lighting.

When speaking to a lighting designer, ask questions. For example, for nighttime scenes, ask whether they plan to use a deep Blue. Ask specifically about special moments and what the lighting designer may have planned. Please specify what **you** have planned for special moments if you intend them to be anything specific. And, be willing to look carefully during first dress rehearsal and ask for adjustments, if needed, right away. Stage lighting will have a major impact on how costumes look and how color is perceived. The lighting designer can be an ally – take the time to understand their language and to discuss ideas with them.

RECOMMENDED BOOKS

This book represents ideas developed over decades of working as a costume designer, but there have been several books that I find myself returning to again and again:

Allen, Jeanne, *Showing Your Colors: A Designer's Guide to Coordinating Your Wardrobe* (ASIN: B004DYSCVS), Chronicle Books, 1986

Two-, three-, and four-color combinations are shown in the context of simple outfits. The text discusses why colors do or do not work well together. The illustrations show the era of the 1980s, and color trends may have changed since the book was published, but presenting color combinations on figures remains a very useful way for a designer to become more sensitive to which colors appear harmonious or not to them within the context of garments on the human figure.

A Designer's Guide to Color series, 1–5:
Shibukawa, Ikuyoshi and Yumi Takahashi, *A Designer's Guide to Color, 1* (ISBN-13: 978-0811857048), Chronicle Books, illustrated edition, 2006

Shibukawa, Ikuyoshi and Yumi Takahashi, *A Designer's Guide to Color, 2* (ISBN-13: 978-0811857284), Chronicle Books, illustrated edition, 2006

Haishoku, Ikuyoshi and Jiten Shibukawa, *A Designer's Guide to Color, 3* (ISBN-13: 978-8770140867), Chronicle Books, 2006

Shibukawa, Ikuyoshi and Yumi Takahashi, *A Designer's Guide to Color, 4* (ISBN-13: 978-0811857093), Chronicle Books, 2006

Shibukawa, Ikuyoshi and Yumi Takahashi, *A Designer's Guide to Color, 5* (ISBN-13: 978-0877018780), Chronicle Books, 2006

These books are available as a boxed set or as individual volumes. The text is in English. Although originally created in the early 1990s, there is a 2nd edition published in 2006. The color schemes are a good starting point for using according to the suggestions in *A Working Costume Designer's Guide to Color.*

INDEX

References to figures are indicated in *italics*.

95–100, *95–100*; defining 18; and
Dominant/Supporting/Accent
Color Schemes 79, 81, 83; and visual
inspiration sources 8, 118; Yellow (high-
Value) and Blue (low-Value) *19*
visual sources: creating color schemes from
8, 73–74, 118–119, 123; London spiral
example *74*, 119, *120–121*, 119–120,
122–123, 121, *124*; Proportional colors
8, 73–74, 118–119, 123, *125–126*;
working with design team 121
"Voice of Reason" characters: and costume
color choices 141
"Voice of the community" groupings: and
costume color choices 141–142; *see also*
choruses

The Waiting Room (Lisa Loomer) 3, *5*
Wallace, Naomi: *The Trestle at Pope Lick
Creek* 7
Warm Colors *67, 67*, 84, 92, 161; *see also*
Color Temperature
wealth/status (of characters): and costume
color choices 138, 140, 190
West Side Story 3
White: with Accent Colors *35*; added as
Accents 59, *60*; "all-White" costume
design 29; Black, Grey, and White color
range *1*; and color distribution process

186, 187; and color temperature *88*;
Neutral color 21, *22*; and One-Hue
(Monochromatic) schemes *35*; "Show
White" 186; and Tints 30, 40, 64, 104;
and True Monochromatic 30, *30*;
and Two-Color (Bi-chromatic) color
schemes 46, *46*; *see also* color meanings
White light 25, 229–230, 231–232
work lights 231

Yellow: in Broad Monochromatic *31*;
and color temperature 87; in Double
Complementary Schemes *57, 58*;
with Green added on computer to
subdue colors *21*; with Grey added on
computer to create Tone *21*; inherently
high-Value 18, *19*; opposing "stacks" of
color on costumes *33*; in Partial triad
combinations *44, 45*; as Primary Color
24, 25; in Split Complementary color
schemes *56, 57*; in Triad combinations
48; in Triad combinations (Altered
Analogous colors) *53, 54*; in Triad
combinations (Pure Analogous colors)
50, 51; in True Complementary
color schemes *38, 39*; in Unequal
Complement schemes *41, 43*; Warm
Colors based on 67, 84; *see also* color
meanings